Workshop about Language Resources for the SSH Cloud (LR4SSHOC 2020)

Marseille, France
11 – 16 May 2020

Editors:

Daan Broeder
Maria Eskevich
Monica Monachini

ISBN: 978-1-7138-1267-8

Printed from e-media with permission by:

Curran Associates, Inc.
57 Morehouse Lane
Red Hook, NY 12571

Some format issues inherent in the e-media version may also appear in this print version.

Association for Computational Linguistics
209 N. Eighth Street
Stroudsburg, Pennsylvania 18360

Phone: 1-570-476-8006
Fax: 1-570-476-0860

acl@aclweb.org

Additional copies of this publication are available from:

Curran Associates, Inc.
57 Morehouse Lane
Red Hook, NY 12571 USA
Phone: 845-758-0400
Fax: 845-758-2633
Email: curran@proceedings.com
Web: www.proceedings.com

LREC 2020 Workshop
Language Resources and Evaluation Conference
11–16 May 2020

Workshop about Language Resources for the SSH Cloud (LR4SSHOC)

PROCEEDINGS

Editors: Daan Broeder, Maria Eskevich, Monica Monachini

Proceedings of the LREC 2020 Workshop about Language Resources for the SSH Cloud (LR4SSHOC)

Edited by: Daan Broeder, Maria Eskevich, and Monica Monachini

Acknowledgements: This workshop is supported through funding from European Union's Horizon 2020 research and innovation programme (under grant agreement No 823782 for the SSHOC project) and the CLARIN infrastructure.

Workshop web site: https://www.clarin.eu/LR4SSHOC

For more information:
European Language Resources Association (ELRA)
9 rue des Cordelières
75013, Paris
France
http://www.elra.info
Email: lrec@elda.org

Introduction

In recent decades the development of language resources (LR) and language technologies (LT) and their management have reached the level of maturity that allows their usage to be expanded beyond the borders of traditional linguistic disciplines and implementations. Although admittedly many challenges remain such as easier localisation, configuration and deployment of LT services for non LT experts.

At the same time, the broad domain of social sciences and humanities (SSH) research despite having a diverse set of domain specific methods and practices, can benefit from LT infrastructure approaches and research results, to extract information from natural language content. These LT methods and practices can be adopted by the already existing SSH research infrastructures that support their domain specific work. And In the larger context, on the European landscape level, the European Open Science Cloud (EOSC), currently under development, will be created to also facilitate the cross domain use of data and technologies. To support this strategy, a set of EU thematic cluster projects collects common and specific requests from kindred fields and domains to ensure a smooth transition and collaboration in order to reach the goal of bringing data, tools and services into the common cloud. The Social Sciences and Humanities Open Cloud (SSHOC) project is the SSH thematic cluster project aiming to create the SSH part of the EOSC.

This workshop was envisaged to focus on the goals and aims of realising the SSHOC part of the EOSC, where SSH data, language processing tools, and services are made available, adjusted and accessible for users across SSH domain. It provides a forum to discuss common requirements, challenges and opportunities for developing, enhancing, integrating tools and services for managing and processing SSH research data. Such SSH scenarios based implementations of currently existing language tools and services demonstrate their multidisciplinary usability and stimulate further multidisciplinary collaboration across the various subfields of SSH and beyond, which will increase the potential for societal impact.

The workshop introduces the SSHOC project and its ambitions while also including its embedding in the EOSC for dialogue with the LREC community. On the one hand, such discussion between SSH data-practitioners, infrastructure and LT experts will strengthen and support the SSH community connection with the LREC landscape and initiatives. On the other hand, the much increased interest in and availability of cloud type infrastructure approaches represent an opportunity for the language technologies to support the field of social sciences and humanities on a large scale following the F.A.I.R. principles, thus supporting its replicability and reproducibility.

For this workshop we have ask for contributions aimed at aligning and integrating services and infrastructure from the Social Sciences, Humanities and Cultural Heritage with one another and with the now emerging European Open Science Cloud, that is being built for sharing and optimising research data and services in a sustainable way. It is especially interesting to see the examples of such infrastructure components that (can) play a role in this, but also at use-cases of cross-domain use of SSH services.

This workshop aimed at gathering together academics, industrial researchers, digital language resources and technology providers, software developers, but also, and in particular, SSH representatives in order to identify the current capacity and the difficulties in creating and sustaining an infrastructure for SSH domain.

The accepted papers address the following topics:

- Research infrastructure components
- Use cases of text and data mining for SSH-driven tasks

- FAIRness of sensitive language data
- Challenges for language technologies in EOSC
- SSH future and governance in the EOSC world
- EOSC and business models for language data, tools and services

The workshop programme is composed of 4 invited papers and 5 peer-reviewed papers. We would like to thank the reviewers for their careful and constructive reviews which have contributed to the quality of the event.

Due to the COVID-19 pandemic, the main conference is postponed, and consequently, the LR4SSHOC workshop is postponed till later possibility to gather the audience of authors and invited speakers.

D. Broeder, M. Eskevich, M. Monachini, M. Kleemola, N. Larrousse May 2020

Organizers:

Daan Broeder, CLARIN ERIC
Maria Eskevich, CLARIN ERIC
Monica Monachini, Institute of Computational Linguistics - CNR
Mari Kleemola, TAU, CESSDA-FI
Nicolas Larrousse, Huma-num, DARIAH-FR, CLARIN-FR

Program Committee:

Daan Broeder, CLARIN ERIC, The Netherlands
Maria Eskevich, CLARIN ERIC, The Netherlands
Vasso Kalaitzi, LIBER, The Netherlands
Mari Kleemola, TAU, CESSDA-FI
Nicolas Larrousse, Huma-num, DARIAH-FR, CLARIN-FR, France
Monica Monachini, Institute of Computational Linguistics - CNR
Jan Odijk, Utrecht University, The Netherlands

Invited Contributors:

Daan Broeder, Maria Eskevich, CLARIN ERIC
Donatella Castelli, Istituto di Scienza e Tecnologie dell'Informazione "A. Faedo", Consiglio Nazionale delle Ricerche
Christopher Cieri, University of Pennsylvania, Linguistic Data Consortium
Henk van den Heuvel, CLS/CLST, Radboud University
Monica Monachini, Institute of Computational Linguistics - CNR

Workshop Program

Peer-reviewed papers

Invited position papers

Proceedings of LR4SSHOC: Workshop about Language Resources for the SSH Cloud, pages 1–4
Language Resources and Evaluation Conference (LREC 2020), Marseille, 11–16 May 2020

Store Scientific Workflows in SSHOC Repository

Cesare Concordia, Carlo Meghini, Filippo Benedetti
CNR - ISTI
Area della Ricerca CNR, via G. Moruzzi 1, 56124 Pisa, Italy
{cesare.concordia, carlo.meghini, filippo.benedetti}@isti.cnr.it

Abstract

Today scientific workflows are used by scientists as a way to define automated, scalable, and portable in-silico experiments. Having a formal description of an experiment can improve replicability and reproducibility of the experiment. However, simply publishing the workflow may be not enough to achieve reproducibility and re-usability, in particular workflow description should be enriched with provenance data generated during the workflow life cycle. This paper presents a software framework being designed and developed in the context of the Social Sciences and Humanities Open Cloud (SSHOC) project, whose overall objective is to realise the social sciences and humanities' part of European Open Science Cloud initiative. The framework will implement functionalities to use the SSHOC Repository service as a cloud repository for scientific workflows.

- **Keywords:** Research infrastructure components, scientific workflows, reproducibility

1. Introduction

Workflows were initially used in the business environment as a way to describe the flow of activities through an organization and were later adopted also for scientific applications. Today scientific workflows (Qin and Fahringer, 2012) are used by scientists as a way to define automated, scalable, and portable in-silico experiments. In recent years a number of studies have been made concerning the use of workflows in the Social Sciences and Humanities (SSH) scientific community (Turner and Lambert, 2015; Matthew and Shapiro, 2014). These studies, starting from the consideration that most SSH researchers create or reuse scripts (written in such programming languages as R, Python, Haskell etc) in their activities, introduce approaches on how to build scientific workflows for complex experiments, starting from these scripts. A researcher can consider scripts as building blocks and use a Workflow Management Systems (WMS) to: relate scripts using graphical notation, execute them, access and manage data, monitor processes and analyse results. In most cases it is not required a strong technical skill to build scientific workflows (Turner and Lambert, 2015), scripts can be seen as black boxes having input parameters and producing outputs, the user relies on the WMS functionalities to deal with many technical details. Scientific workflows are considered a way for researchers to formally describe complex scientific experiments, and it is becoming a widely adopted practice among researchers to publish scientific workflows, alongside with datasets, in order to enable reproducibility and replicability of experiments.

The Social Sciences and Humanities Open Cloud (SSHOC) project[1] aims at realising the transition from the current SSH landscape with separated e-infrastructure facilities into a cloud-based infrastructure offering a scalable and flexible model of access to research data and related services adapted to the needs of the SSH scientific community. In particular the project will generate services for optimal re-use of data by making data Findable, Accessible, Interoperable and Re-usable (FAIR). In this context it is important to provide a service enabling researchers to publish scientific workflows to enable reproducibility of experiments.

This paper describes a software framework that is being designed and implemented in the SSHOC project, to enable scientists and researchers in the SSH domains to use the SSHOC Repository as a repository for publishing the scientific workflows used in their experiments. The document first presents an overview of scientific workflows, then reports the major guidelines suggested in scientific literatures for storing and publishing workflows and in its last part presents the frameworks being developed.

2. Scientific Workflows Overview

A scientific workflow is a composition of interconnected and possibly heterogeneous scripts that are used in a scientific experiment. Scientific workflow languages provide statements to define the logic that relates calls of scripts; for certain processes, such as statistical analysis, a linear flow might be sufficient, but more complex flows may allow for parallel execution, event handling, compensation handling and error handling. According to (Barga and Digiampietri, 2008) a scientific workflow may be considered as a way to record the origins of a result, how it is obtained, experimental methods used, machine calibrations and parameters, etc. Examples of scientific workflows are: data chaining pipelines that gather and merges data from multiple sources, sequence of steps automating repetitive tasks (e.g. data access, data transformation), complex iterative chains of MapReduce jobs etc. Scientific workflows are created and managed using specific software frameworks called Scientific Workflow Management Systems (SWMS). An SWMS implements the execution of the scripts, manages the allocation of computational resources and the input and output of data ("data staging"), deploys software, cleans up

[1] https://sshopencloud.eu

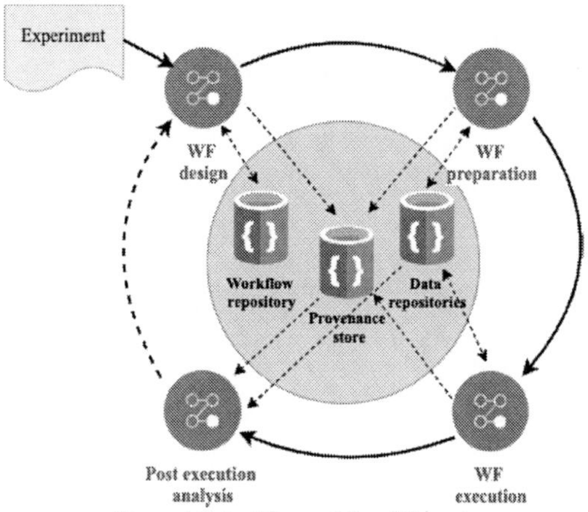

Figure 1 Scientific workflow life cycle

temporary data etc. Examples of SWMS are Kepler[2] and Taverna[3]. The life cycle of scientific workflows is composed of four main phases (Ludäscher et al, 2009): design, preparation, execution and post-execution analysis.

During the design and preparation phases, researchers may want to reuse pre-existing workflows (partly or as a whole) to create the new workflow. The SWMS provides functionalities to access local or remote[4] *workflow repositories*.

During execution phase, existing datasets are processed and new datasets can be generated. These datasets are accessed/stored by scripts, but the SWMS tracks these operations, and if necessary activates compensation handling procedures.

Every phase of a workflow life cycle generates provenance data, it is important to collect this data and store it. Provenance data of scientific workflows represents the entire history of the derivation of the final output of a workflow (Tan, 2007), it includes global configuration parameters, data propagation, data provenance of scripts, user annotations, performance and memory footprint etc. This data is used in the post-execution analysis phase: researchers evaluate data products and provenance information in order to validate the experiment. Provenance data is crucial to improve the reproducibility of workflows (Simmhan et al 2005), (Deelman et al. 2018).

3. Publishing Scientific Workflows

In principle, having a formal description of an experiment as a workflow (or as a script) can improve replicability and reproducibility of the experiments[5]:

- reproducibility: obtaining consistent computational results using the same input data, computational steps, methods, code, and conditions of analysis.
- replicability: obtaining consistent results across studies aimed at answering the same scientific question, each of which has obtained its own data.

According to the above definitions, reproducing experiments involves using the original data and code, while replicating it involves new data collection and similar methods used by previous studies. Today it is an established behaviour in scientific communities to publish datasets used in experiments alongside with the scripts or workflows developed to process the datasets. However, according to many studies, this practice may not be sufficient to guarantee re-usability of datasets and reproducibility of experiments. This section focuses on issues on reproducibility of scientific workflows.

After February 2011 the journal Science adopted a policy that requires researchers to fulfil all reasonable requests for the data and code needed to generate results published in their papers. In a study, (Stodden et al. 2018) tested the reproducibility of results from a random sample of 204 scientific papers published in the journal after February 2011; they obtained data, scripts or workflows for 89 articles in their sample, and results could only be reproduced (with some efforts) for 56 articles, about 27% of total. In his study (Chen 2018) analysed all datasets published from 2015 to 2018 in the Harvard Dataverse[6] containing R scripts to reproduce results. His work concludes that 85.6% of stored R programs, when re-executed, generate several kinds of 'fatal' errors; only a subset of scripts runs correctly after debugging operations, while a significant number of scripts remains not usable. According to both studies a major reason for the reproducibility issues is the lack of provenance data, especially the lack information about the computational context of the scripts: library or external software packages dependencies, specific datasets versions, random or pseudo-random input values, etc.

The importance of capturing and storing provenance data to improve reproducibility of e-science experiments is outlined in several studies. In particular (Deelman et al.) clearly states that provenance data is necessary for reproducibility of scientific workflows.

4. The SSHOC Repository

One of the goals of SSHOC is to provide an European Open Science Cloud[7] (EOSC) repository service. An EOSC service can be defined as a resource that provide EOSC System Users with ready-to-use facilities. EOSC Services are supplied by a Service Provider in

[2]https://www.cct.lsu.edu/~sidhanti/classes/csc7700/papers/Ledashner05.pdf

[3]https://onlinelibrary.wiley.com/doi/full/10.1002/cpe.1235

[4] E.g. myexperiment.org

[5]https://sites.nationalacademies.org/sites/reproducibility-in-science/index.htm

[6] https://dataverse.harvard.edu

[7] https://www.eosc-portal.eu

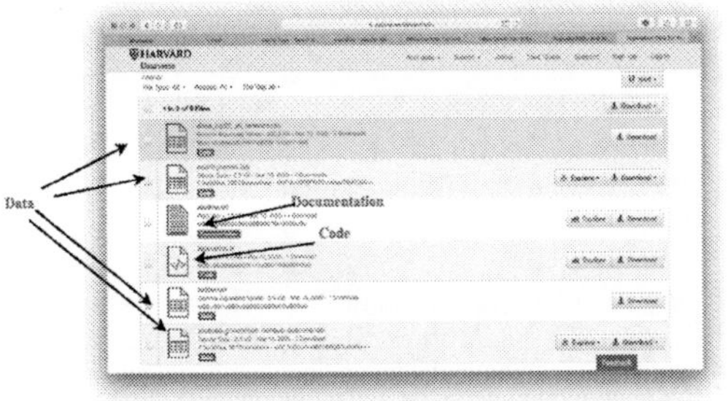

Figure 2 Example of datasets and scripts published in Harvard Dataverse

accordance with the Rules of Participation for EOSC Service Providers[8]. The SSHOC EOSC Repository service will provide SSH institutions without a repository service, such a facility for their designated communities. For organizations with limited technical resources, the service offers an opportunity to simply and effectively create an online repository. For organizations, which already provide archival solutions, this service can be used to set up a sharing and self-depositing environment for researchers in a user-centric manner.

The SSHOC EOSC Repository service is built upon the Dataverse software. The Dataverse is an open source web application designed to share, preserve, cite, explore, and analyse research data. Dataverse development is being coordinated by the Harvard's Institute for Quantitative Social Science (IQSS)[9]. Dataverse provides (among others) the following functionalities:

- A data citation with a persistent identifier (DOI)
- Standard metadata, plus custom metadata for journals
- Tiered access to data as needed: Fully Open, CC0, Register to access; Guestbook, Restricted
- Anonymous dataset review
- Versioning of datasets
- FAIR principles support
- Support for provenance (under development)[10]

Moreover, Dataverse allows integrations with other data services such as DataCite or ROpenScience. A Dataverse repository is a software installation, which hosts multiple virtual archives called *dataverses*. Each dataverse can contain several datasets, and each dataset contains descriptive metadata, code and data files. The Dataverse architecture implements the Service Oriented Architecture (SOA) principles, and provides APIs that can be used by developers to integrate micro-services on top. This last feature will be used as entry point for the software framework developed in this activity.

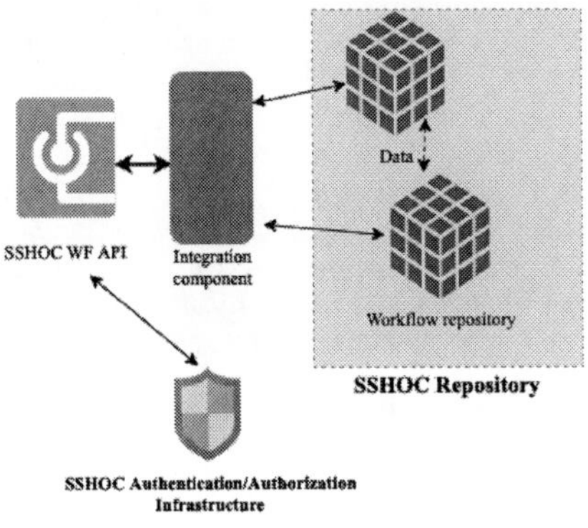

Figure 3 Overall architecture of SSHOC Workflow Repository API

5. The SSHOC Workflow Repository API

The SSHOC Workflow Repository API is a software framework that can enable an SWFMS to use the SSHOC Repository as a workflow repository.

This software will implement a set of functionalities that can enable an SSH researcher to use the SSHOC Repository as

- a repository where to store and publish workflows alongside witjh the datasets used in her/his research
- a workflow repository that can be browsed and searched, for instance to re-use stored workflows in the design phase of new scientific workflows

Technically speaking the software will be composed of two main components (Fig. 3): an API publishing functionalities as Web Services and a middleware implementing the integration layer with the SSHOC Repository. A client application can use the SSHOC WF API to enable users to access workflows, download them, and execute or reuse to build new workflows.

A key challenge of the work is the definition of a data model for representing workflows. The general idea is to investigate a correct way to 'enrich' workflows description to improve both reproducibility of experiments and reusability of workflow as part of other workflows. As previously discussed data provenance has the potential to address a number of reproducibility issues. Provenance data for scientific workflows are collected by SWMS (observed provenance) and stored in local repositories or log files. The data provenance is currently mainly used to monitor the workflows behaviour and to enable an

[8] https://www.eosc-portal.eu/glossary

[9] https://www.iq.harvard.edu/product-development

[10] https://projects.iq.harvard.edu/provenance-at-harvard/tools

accurate post execution analysis. However, at the moment there is not yet a standard data provenance model for workflows (Delman et al. 2018), therefore in the first phase we have started to investigate the main approaches followed such as OPMW[11] or D-OPM (Cuevas-Vicenttín et al, 2012). They are based on W3C Open Provenance Model specification and describes workflows as graphs whose nodes are tasks and edges are relationships between tasks. These models provide very few specifications for provenance data and this could be an issue.

The SWMS Apache Taverna will be used to create a reference implementation for a client of the SSHOC WF API.

The Apache Taverna is an open source and domain-independent Scientific Workflow Management System, the data model used by Taverna is compatible with the W3C Open Provenance Model.

In particular there will be developed a plugin to enable Taverna Workbench users to use the SSHOC Repository. The Taverna Workbench is a tool that enables users to create, configure, execute and manage Taverna workflows, using a GUI. It is designed as a plugin platform, this means that its functionalities can be extended by installing new plugins.

The Taverna-SSHOC Repository plugin will be initially internally used to test developed software, and in a later stage it will be released via a public Maven repository to enable SSH scientists using Taverna to use its functionalities. The SSHOC WF Repository API and the plugin will be developed using Java based technologies.

6. Conclusion

This paper has presented a software framework for enabling SSH researchers to use the SSHOC Repository to store and publish scientific workflows. The software framework will technical implement the integration layer between the SSHOC Repository and a generic SWMSs, thus enabling users to store and access workflows, improving reproducibility of experiments and re-use of code. This activity is in progress: the design of the software is completed and design documents is going to be released in the following months. A first (alpha) release of the SSHOC WF API has been developed and deployed on development servers and is currently being tested. Technical documentation of the Web Services are available on line[12] while the source code will be published on SSHOC development repository.

7. Bibliographical References

Bertram Ludäscher, Mathias Weske, Timothy McPhillips, and Shawn Bowers. Scientific workflows: Business as usual?,7th Intl. Conf. on Business Process Management (BPM), LNCS 5701, Ulm, Germany, 2009 DOI: 10.1007/978-3-642-03848-8_4

Chen, Christopher Coding Be eR: Assessing and Improving the Reproducibility of R-Based Research With containR (2018). http://nrs.harvard.edu/urn-3:HUL.InstRepos:38811561

Deelman, E., Peterka, T., Altintas, I., Carothers, C. D., van Dam, K. K., Moreland, K., … Vetter, J. (2018). The future of scientific workflows. The International Journal of High Performance Computing Applications, 32(1), 159–175. https://doi.org/10.1177/1094342017704893

Gentzkow, Matthew and Jesse M. Shapiro. “Code and Data for the Social Sciences: A Practitioner's Guide.” (2014).

J. Qin and T. Fahringer, editors. Scientific Workflows – Programming, Optimization, and Synthesis with ASKALON and AWDL. Springer, Berlin, Germany, Aug. 2012.

Record, 34(3):31, 2005.

Roger S. Barga Luciano A. Digiampietri Automatic capture and efficient storage of e-Science experiment provenance. Concurrency Computat.: Pract. Exper. 2008; 20:419–429

Simmhan Y L, Plale B, and Gannon D. A survey of data provenance in e-science. ACM SIGMOD

T. Pasquier, M. K. Lau, X. Han, E. Fong, B. S. Lerner, E. Boose, M. Crosas, A. Ellison, and M. Seltzer, “Sharing and Preserving Computational Analyses for Posterity with encapsulator,” ArXiv e-prints, Mar. 2018.

Tan, W. C. Provenance in Databases: Past, Current, and Future. IEEE Data Engineering Bulletin, 30(4):3–12, Dec. 2007.

Turner, K.J., Lambert, P.S. Workflows for quantitative data analysis in the social sciences. Int J Softw Tools Technol Transfer 17, 321–338 (2015). https://doi.org/10.1007/s10009-014-0315-4

V. Cuevas-Vicenttín, S. Dey, M. L. Y. Wang, T. Song and B. Ludäscher, "Modeling and Querying Scientific Workflow Provenance in the D-OPM," 2012 SC Companion: High Performance Computing, Networking Storage and Analysis, Salt Lake City, UT, 2012, pp. 119-128.

V. Stodden, J. Seiler,and Z. Ma, “An empirical analysis of journal policy effectiveness for computational reproducibility,” Proceedings of the National Academy of Sciences, vol. 115, no. 11, pp. 2584–2589, 2018.

[11] https://www.opmw.org

[12] http://146.48.85.197/Dataverse_tool-0.0.1-SNAPSHOT/swagger-ui.html#/

Social Sciences and Humanities Pathway Towards the European Open Science Cloud

Suzanne Dumouchel, Francesca Di Donato, Monica Monachini, Yoann Moranville, Stefanie Pohle, Maria Eskevich
CNRS, Net7, CNR, DARIAH, MWS, CLARIN ERIC
suzanne.dumouchel@huma-num.fr, didonato@netseven.it, monica.monachini@ilc.cnr.it, yoann.moranville@dariah.eu, Pohle@maxweberstiftung.de, maria@clarin.eu

Abstract

The paper describes a journey which starts from various social sciences and humanities (SSH) Research Infrastructures (RI) in Europe and arrives at the comprehensive "ecosystem of infrastructures", namely the European Open Science Cloud (EOSC).
We highlight how the SSH Open Science infrastructures contribute to the goal of establishing the EOSC. First, through the example of OPERAS, the European Research Infrastructure for Open Scholarly Communication in the SSH, to see how its services are conceived to be part of the EOSC and to address the communities' needs. The next two sections highlight collaboration practices between partners in Europe to build the SSH component of the EOSC and a SSH discovery platform, as a service of OPERAS and the EOSC. The last two sections focus on an implementation network dedicated to SSH data *fairification*.

Keywords: SSH, Research Infrastructure, EOSC, data, FAIR

1. Introduction

The EOSC implementation plan (DG Research and Innovation, 2019) is based on a federated model, aiming at creating, stimulating and implementing synergies between existing scientific resources, primarily through the Research Infrastructures (RI), including e-Infrastructures, part of the Horizon 2020 Work Programme. This paper guides through a long journey, articulated in a path which starts from the OPERAS RI, and crosses various Social Sciences and Humanities (SSH) Research Infrastructures in Europe to arrive at the comprehensive "ecosystem of infrastructures", namely the European Open Science Cloud (EOSC). It makes several stops at different crossroads to highlight the steps which contribute to developing SSH research both at European and international levels. By depicting this scenario, we aim at drawing the picture of an ecosystem, the European Open Science Cloud (EOSC).

While the EOSC implementation is a multi-year undertaking which is being addressed in practice in several stages, different European infrastructures are currently engaged in the activities in the field of Open Science in the SSH. Most of them are dealing with data, especially to develop tools and guidelines for researchers to be able to share, use and host data, following the FAIR[1] principles. In all initiatives, needs of collaboration emerge in order to reinforce the links between data and publications, especially regarding Persistent Identifiers (PID), data journals, etc.

This paper highlights how the SSH Open Science infrastructures contribute on various levels to the goal of establishing the EOSC. First, through the example of OPERAS, the European Research Infrastructure for Open Scholarly Communication in the SSH, to see how its services are conceived to be part of the EOSC and to address the communities' needs. Then the paper points out collaboration practices between partners in Europe to build the SSH component of the EOSC (in the context of the SSHOC[2] H2020 project) and a discovery platform specifically conceived as an OPERAS service to be integrated into the EOSC (TRIPLE H2020 project). The last two parts of the paper focus again on collaborations: at a national level, through the EOSC-PILLAR project, and internationally, through an implementation network dedicated to SSH data fairification.

2. Crossroad 1: OPERAS-P and OPERAS

OPERAS-P[3] is a two-year, European Commission-funded project, aiming at the development of OPERAS - Open Scholarly Communication in the European Research Area for Social Sciences and Humanities - as a European Research Infrastructure[4].

OPERAS-P project will develop a protocol and a roadmap for the inclusion of the OPERAS Research Infrastructure

[1] https://www.go-fair.org/fair-principles/

[2] Social Sciences and Humanities Open Cloud project.

[3] H2020-INFRADEV-2019-2. See: https://cordis.europa.eu/project/id/871069.

[4] Created in 2015, OPERAS consortium comprises 40 organisations from 16 countries and is led by a Core Group consisting of 9 members.

services for SSH into the EOSC portal. This protocol will be based on the Rules and Procedures already introduced by the EOSC, while taking into account the work in progress of the SSHOC project. The project will implement some of the following OPERAS innovative services, which will be integrated with the EOSC ecosystem:

a. **OPERAS Discovery service.** The TRIPLE project, described in detail below (see Section 4), will become the OPERAS discovery platform, which will provide access to SSH resources, such as data and relevant publications, researcher profiles as well as project descriptions.
b. **OPERAS certification service.** The Directory of Open Access Books (DOAB), which ensures discoverability of Open Access books and delivers global peer-review certification for funders and libraries, will be redeveloped to become a central service of OPERAS as an open source platform based on DSpace technology. This move is crucial for SSH researchers in the light of Plan S[5] and the global shift towards Open Science in Europe.
c. **OPERAS Metrics service.** The Metrics service collects usage metrics and altmetrics from many different sources (Google Books, Matomo analytics, World reader, etc.) about the usage of monographs. Measures are displayed in a light javascript widget, broken down into types and sources, with links to the description of each measure. Different components complement the service, including a data model, an open source tool suite to provide metrics to the service, a central OPERAS database as well as a dashboard and a javascript widget for visualisation.
d. **OPERAS Publishing Service Portal.** Due to the fragmentation of services and tools, SSH researchers in Europe struggle to define and implement their communication strategy in an uncoordinated communication landscape. The OPERAS-P project will implement a common access point to the publishing services offered by its members. This access point is a web portal listing the relevant services provided by the OPERAS infrastructure nodes and beyond. The portal will help researchers in selecting the appropriate publishing venue and defining their scholarly communication strategy.
e. **OPERAS check-in.** To support a transparent and seamless access to the OPERAS platforms and to external sources of data, the EGI check-in service will be adopted as authentication and authorization service within the OPERAS RI. The service provides an identity and access management solution that facilitates the access to services and resources using the federated authentication mechanisms, thanks to the implementation of Virtual Organisation common for OPERAS services and its users.
f. **OPERAS XML toolbox.** In SSH, the community has to overcome a specific obstacle, i.e. the juxtaposition of two standards: XML JATS, adopted by the academic publishing industry, and XML TEI (Text Encoding Initiative) adopted by the humanities research community for books and digital editions. OPERAS-P will provide tools to achieve interoperability between these two standards.

The innovation part of the OPERAS-P project is aimed at producing a robust, empirically tested and stakeholder-validated foundational body of knowledge relevant for the future development and functioning of OPERAS. This includes the development of sustainable models of governance for infrastructures, business models for open scholarly publishing,/groundbreaking concepts to address the fairification of SSH data, multilingualism, the future of scholarly writing as well as quality assessment of novel research outputs.

In sum, OPERAS-P means a process of transforming OPERAS to the status of a mature community, with a set of services compatible with EOSC, stable national nodes and innovative plans for future development.

3. Crossroad 2: Building the SSH component of the EOSC (SSHOC)

The overall objective of the SSHOC project[6] is to build the SSH component of the EOSC.

The project aims at realising the transition from the current landscape with disciplinary silos and separated e-infrastructure facilities into a cloud-based infrastructure where data are FAIR, and tools and training are available for SSH scholars who have adopted, or want to adopt, a data-driven scientific approach and who have an interest in the innovation and integration of their methodological frameworks.

The ambition of SSHOC is to:

a. Increase the efficiency and productivity of researchers - by providing a fully-fledged SSH Cloud where data, tools and services are easily and seamlessly discoverable, accessible and (re)usable.
b. Contribute to the creation of a cross-border and multi-disciplinary open innovation environment - by fostering the development of infrastructural support for digital scholarship.
c. Strengthen/encourage the collaboration between the partners involved in the SSHOC project that are representing the broad spectrum of the SSH community through the use and harmonisation of different technologies and services that are already available and also being developed within the course of the project.

The project therefore aims for synergies across disciplines and work towards a clustered cloud infrastructure that makes use of common elements, such as secured login, storage and computing power, and other e-infrastructures. The project is very well connected to national activities,

[5] https://www.coalition-s.org/

[6] INFRAEOSC-04-2018, Social Science and Humanities Open Cloud https://www.sshopencloud.eu/about-sshoc.

thanks to the participation of all five SSH ERICs (European Research Infrastructure Consortium). Furthermore, salient pan-European and global data surveys participatie in the project. SSHOC also participates in international activities such as the Research Data Alliance and other initiatives of a similar nature. The SSHOC ecosystem will use the existing infrastructures that are already provided by the project partners and will improve the findability of make existing tools and services for diverse communities of potential use better available. In particular, the SSHOC approach is to develop, enhance, integrate a set of tools and services for managing and processing SSH research data that are central to the communities of use in SSH, based on existing tools and functionalities, and requirements for interoperability. Existing tools and services will be adjusted and enriched, making connections to EOSC-hub e-infrastructure for the sharing and use of tools and services useful for SSH. Special attention is given to cross-disciplinary use of services e.g. providing language technology for social -sciences and humanities scenarios of use.

The SSHOC project will cover the full Research and Development and ready-to-market cycle: in particular, the SSH Open Marketplace platform will contain solutions, training materials, tools and services for researchers, all contextualised within one another. The lack of a central place integrating assets from all SSH-related project websites, service registries and data repositories is what drove the creation of this Marketplace. The choice was made to provide datasets via the Marketplace only when relevant in the context of tools, trainings or other materials[7]. The Marketplace has always, since itsbeginning, been conceptualised as a community-oriented platform where the community can directly take part in the curation of its data. The leveraged services will deeply embed Open Science and FAIR principles by making data Findable, Accessible, Interoperable and Re-usable.

4. Crossroad 3: Building a European discovery service for SSH data (TRIPLE)

SSH research is divided across a wide array of disciplines, sub-disciplines and languages. While this specialisation makes it possible to investigate the extensive variety of SSH topics, it also leads to a fragmentation that prevents SSH research from reaching its full potential. Use and reuse of SSH research is suboptimal, interdisciplinary collaboration possibilities are often missed, and as a result, societal, economic and academic impacts are limited (Dallas C., 2017).

The TRIPLE project[8], which consists of a consortium of currently 19 partners from 13 countries, is a practical answer to the above issues, as it aims at designing and developing a multilingual and multicultural discovery platform dedicated to SSH resources at European scale. TRIPLE will improve the accessibility and dissemination of SSH resources through a single access point which allows free access to circa six million documents in the domain of Social Sciences and Humanities, including peer reviewed journals, articles, books and blog posts, as well as to research data, projects and researcher profiles.

The TRIPLE solution will provide linked exploration thanks to (1) the ISIDORE search engine[9], and (2) a variety of connected innovative tools, which include visualisations, a web annotation service, a trust building system, a crowdfunding system and a recommender system.

TRIPLE main objective is then to enable researchers to discover and reuse SSH data macro-typologies, related not only to publications, but also to people and projects.

The integration of TRIPLE into the EOSC will be performed according to EOSC general principles and to the set of recommendations and guidelines, structured under the six priorities, i.e. Landscape, FAIR, Architecture, Rules of Participation and Sustainability, Skills and Training, which are coordinated by the relative EOSC Working Groups.

A major strength lies in the composition of the TRIPLE consortium: Not only are the main RIs for SSH project partners, but several partners also play an active part in the EOSC implementation. Moreover, specific synergies are developed with SSHOC, and Memorandums of Understanding (starting with SSHOC) are planned.

The TRIPLE solution is envisaged to be a major component of the SSH Open Marketplace, which will be the entry door to the EOSC for all the different SSH services.

The TRIPLE consortium is also experimenting with new forms of engagement and community-building through the TRIPLE Forum, which will bring together relevant stakeholders. Linked to the SSHOC community and the ones served by the Research Infrastructures, TRIPLE Forum will contribute to bringing the researchers into the EOSC and more largely into the Open Science movement.

5. Crossroad 4: Beyond national services, how SSH open collaborations

The EOSC-Pillar project (https://www.eosc-pillar.eu/) aims to identify, coordinate and harmonize existing national initiatives for the national coordination of data

[7] TRIPLE could overcome potential gaps by providing access to other datasets, see https://doi.org/10.5281/zenodo.3547649 and Section 4

[8] Funded under the European Commission program INFRAEOSC-02-2019 "Prototyping new innovative services".

[9] ISIDORE is a large-scale discovery service, developed by the TGIR Huma-Num (CNRS) since 2009 (https://isidore.science/).

infrastructures and services that recently started in many Member States (MS) as one of the founding pillars for the development and the long-term sustainability of the EOSC. The idea is, thus, leveraging national initiatives of the MS and Thematic Initiatives (TI) developed by research communities working in national and European collaborations to build a future based on Open Science and FAIR data practices.

Concretely, that implies to:

a. Support the coordination and harmonization of mature national initiatives for open data, open science services, cloud and data infrastructures.
b. Facilitate the adoption and compliance with EOSC standards… while proactively providing feedback to the EOSC governance…
c. Contribute to the creation of an achievable cutting-edge, end user-oriented environment for European data-driven science, through the promotion of FAIR practices and services.

The Federation of National Initiatives will be the catalyst for trans-national open data and open science services (common policies, FAIR services, shared standards, technical choices). The project gathers representatives of the fast-growing national initiatives for coordinating data infrastructures and services in Italy, France, Germany, Austria and Belgium. In this framework, the French Very Large Research Infrastructure Huma-Num and the Center for Direct Scientific Communication (CCSD), who created the HAL open archive and is now in charge of its development and management, together with the conference management platform SciencesConf.org and the hosting platform of epi-journals, decided to join their effort to propose a Proof of Concept (POC) around two of their services for SSH. This POC will link the Huma-Num repository NAKALA to the HAL open archive to address the need for SSH to be able to prove the authenticity of data, and to guarantee accessibility to raw data which are at the root of research and innovation - this approach being in a perspective of reproducibility of the research.

In EOSC-Pillar, the SSH community is built from regional areas. It highlights practices and opens opportunities for new collaborations with other disciplines, so as to bring researchers to new networks and innovative research projects.

6. Crossroad 5: Beyond the EOSC, implementing SSH data FAIRification

CO-OPERAS is an Implementation Network within the context of the GoFAIR initiative (https://www.go-fair.org/implementation-networks/overview/co-operas/). It aims to bring SSH data into the EOSC, helping communities to FAIRifying them, and, in turn, to enrich the FAIRification process and registries with specific SSH standards. "Define FAIR for implementation" is also the first Recommendation of the DG Research and Innovation, 2018.

The network was created and launched in 2019, and is one of OPERAS' building blocks connecting European and international research communities through the FAIR principles as a common ground. In that sense, within the OPERAS environment, CO-OPERAS' activities represent a reciprocal movement towards and from the research infrastructure: on the one hand, it brings feedback and suggestions from specific communities in order to implement the services; on the other hand it brings coordination to fragmented and heterogeneous communities.

CO-OPERAS stands right at the crossroad between data and publications, and it perfectly fits in the OPERAS ecosystem as it more than integrates data and publications. As a community-based network, CO-OPERAS' first aim is to define the term "data" in the field of SSH. To this purpose, regional and national workshops in different languages (e.g. Italian, German, French…) are being organized. Researchers are asked to provide their definitions of "data", and then to assess the level of FAIRness maturity of the data they are using and creating. Diversity comes along with fragmentation of practices and lack of standards. Then, the SSH community needs to converge around shared expertise and practices. To do so, the FAIR principles are one of the most valuable tools as they are able to be broadly applied and widely shared.

Identifying the gaps and the critical issues is crucial in order to plan new useful services or to create new standards and promote their adoption. In parallel, OPERAS' services and related projects such as TRIPLE and SSHOC will offer a field of application for concrete and improved FAIR data curation, discovery, harvesting, and reuse in the SSH.

7. Conclusions

Building EOSC components implies to be well-organised and coordinated at a European scale. For the Social Sciences and the Humanities, often fragmented also from a linguistic point of view, the challenge is quite high.

The above surveyed initiatives focus each both on general and on specific aspects which, in the end, contribute to define a set of rules and guidelines for the implementation of the SSH components of the EOSC.

This is why there is a strong need for collaborations between European Research Infrastructures, as well as for interoperability of the services. But what is most important is to share a common goal and to work in the same direction.

In general, strong synergies are in place between all the described initiatives and projects:

- the main RIs for SSH, i.e. CLARIN, DARIAH and CESSDA, are TRIPLE project members, and all the five

ERICs (the three above plus SHARE and ESS) are SSHOC project members;

- specific synergies are developed between TRIPLE and SSHOC, where the coordinator (CESSDA) is a TRIPLE partner, and CNRS and CNR are SSHOC partners;

- Memorandums of Understanding are planned;

- EGI partnership within TRIPLE ensures that the technology will be fully interoperable with other e-infrastructures services, especially regarding AAI technology and resource discoverability;

- the collaboration between TRIPLE, SSHOC and the CO-OPERAS Implementation Network, in which, respectively, 12 TRIPLE partners and 3 SSHOC partners are part of, builds a bridge between SSH data and the EOSC, widening the concept of "research data" to all types of digital SSH research outputs;

- numerous discussions about the EOSC are linked to FAIRification of data, in the STM[10] especially focusing on big data. In the SSH field, data does not always fit the definition of "big data", but it still requires specific management and solutions. The CO-OPERAS work on SSH fairification, and specifically on FAIR Implementation Profiles and FAIR Data Objects, can be relevant for SSH initiatives.

SSH contribution to the EOSC definition and implementation draws upon the strong efforts made within the different projects and initiatives to build a strong SSH community. Within the SSH, communities of practice are very fragmented but with a high willingness to share practices and knowledge and to build upon the existing commonalities. Links are strengthened between humanities, social sciences, cultural heritage, scholarly communication communities.

All the above described initiatives show a common vision and complementarity while sharing common challenges, such as overcoming fragmentation and the lack of a single, central solution, addressing common issues such as multilingualism, interoperability, fairification, the EOSC marketplace, language and discovery services, and the connection to national and international activities..

These different initiatives could overlap in their activities at some point. However, this is not an issue. SSH are well-known for their diversity of interpretation and their critical dimensions. What is presented in this paper is a federation of SSH facets which contribute to avoid simplification and reduction in order to deploy complexity at a large scale through the different initiatives. This is where SSH, thanks and through the multiple facets, can play a strong role in the building of the EOSC: they anchor a practice in a history, in an area, in a future.

9. Acknowledgements

The work presented in this paper has been partly supported by INFRAEOSC-02-2019 TRIPLE, Transforming Research through Innovative Practices for Linked interdisciplinary Exploration, and partly by INFRAEOSC-04-2018 SSHOC, Social Science and Humanities Open Cloud.

10. Bibliographical References

Burgelman J-C, Pascu C, Szkuta K, Von Schomberg R, Karalopoulos A, Repanas K and Schouppe M (2019) Open Science, Open Data, and Open Scholarship: European Policies to Make Science Fit for the Twenty-First Century. *Front. Big Data* 2:43. doi: 10.3389/fdata.2019.00043.

Barbot L, Moranville Y, Fischer F, Petitfils C, Ďurčo M, Illmayer K, … Karampatakis S (2019). SSHOC D7.1 System Specification - SSH Open Marketplace (Version 1.0). Zenodo, 10.5281/zenodo.3547648.the

Directorate-General for Research and Innovation (2018). Turning FAIR into reality, 1-78, European Commission, Brussels, 978-92-79-96546-3, doi: 10.2777/1524.

Directorate-General for Research and Innovation (2019) European Open Science Cloud (EOSC) strategic implementation plan, 1-48, European Commission, Brussels, 978-92-76-09175-2, doi: 10.2777/202370.

OPERAS Consortium. (2018, July 30). OPERAS Design Study. Zenodo. http://doi.org/10.5281/zenodo.1324055

Von Schomberg, R. (2019). "Why responsible innovation?" in *International Handbook on Responsible Innovation A Global Resource*, eds R. Von Schomberg and J. Hankins (Cheltenham: Edward Elgar Publishing), 12–32. doi: 10.4337/9781784718862 .

Wenger, Etienne (1998). Communities of Practice: Learning, Meaning, and Identity. Cambridge: Cambridge University Press;

Wenger, Etienne; McDermott, Richard; Snyder, William M. (2002). Cultivating Communities of Practice (Hardcover). Harvard Business Press; 1st edition.

[10] Scientific, Technical and Medical sciences

Proceedings of LR4SSHOC: Workshop about Language Resources for the SSH Cloud, pages 10–18
Language Resources and Evaluation Conference (LREC 2020), Marseille, 11–16 May 2020

From the attic to the cloud: mobilization of endangered language resources with linked data

Sebastian Nordhoff
Leibniz-Zentrum Allgemeine Sprachwissenschaft (ZAS Berlin)
Schützenstr. 18, 10117 Berlin
nordhoff@leibniz-zas.de

Abstract

As an important example of the need to provide hosting and publication facilities for highly specific data types and the role thematic centres can play, this paper describes a collection of 20k ELAN annotation files harvested from five different endangered language archives. The ELAN files form a very heterogeneous set, but the hierarchical configuration of their tiers allow, in conjunction with the tier content, to identify transcriptions, translations, and glosses. These transcriptions, translations, and glosses are queryable across archives. Small analyses of graphemes (transcription tier), grammatical and lexical glosses (gloss tier), and semantic concepts (translation tier) show the viability of the approach. The use of identifiers from OLAC, Wikidata and Glottolog allows for a better integration of the data from these archives into the Linguistic Linked Open Data Cloud.

Keywords: endangered languages, corpus, ELAN, text mining, Linked Data

1. Introduction

One of the goals of linguistics is to gain insight into human cognition and culture. There are over 7 000 languages spoken in the world (Hammarström et al., 2019), varying wildly in structure, so we must have a large and diverse sample in order to gain any meaningful insight into what all human languages have in common. The amount of data to process is too large for one human brain, so that machine support is required. Unfortunately, NLP largely focuses on a very small number of languages spoken in the industrialized world. The wiki of the Association for Computational Linguistics lists NLP tools for 76 different languages,[1] i.e. about 1% of the worlds languages. It is true that there are text, audio, and video resources in other languages available, but these are often small, difficult to access, and even more difficult to reuse. Many of the resources for these lesser studied languages reside in endangered language archives such as TLA,[2] ELAR,[3] or PARADISEC.[4] While much of the content found in these archives is available for inspection in principle, there are significant issues of findability and interoperability, rendering its exploitation for NLP purposes difficult. This paper describes a workflow to identify, colllect and query the resources from five different endangered language archives from the DELAMAN network, giving access to 2 500 000 words in a structured format.

2. DELAMAN archives

DELAMAN (Digital Endangered Languages and Musics Archives Network) "is an international network of archives of data on linguistic and cultural diversity, in particular on small languages and cultures under pressure" (www.delaman.org). As such, DELAMAN is a very interesting starting point for the collection of processable resources for lesser studied languages. There are currently 12 member archives and 5 associated members, which hold content in 2420 different languages. For the purpose of this project, 5 archives were chosen for inclusion:

- AILLA (Archive of the Indigenous Languages of Latin America)
- ANLA (Alaska Native Language Archive)
- ELAR (Endangered Languages Archive at SOAS)
- PARADISEC (Pacific and Regional Archive for Digital Sources in Endangered Cultures)
- TLA (The Language Archive at the Max Planck Institute for Psycholinguistics)

These archives vary in size, backend software, funding structure, and coverage of geographical areas. They have in common that their main focus has been on ingestion, and less so on mobilization. There are some query interfaces to identify resources of interest, but none of the archives offers an API or bulk downloads for instance.

3. Research with language archives: *The Language Archive* at the Max Planck Institute for Psycholinguistics

TLA used to be the "home archive" for the DoBeS programm (funded by the Volkswagen foundation), which funded 67 documentation projects for endangered languages. The last project funded started in 2011. In the course of these documentation projects, very interesting and important language data was collected and deposited in the archive. To this day, the researchers from these projects continue using the archive, still funded by the Max Planck Society. However, it is also true that there are only very few "third party" researchers, not involved in the original projects, which interact with the data. The Volkswagen foundation initiated so called phase-2 projects for theoretical research on language data stored in the archive, but only 5 such projects[5] have been awarded and as of today there seems to be no major research community interacting with archive data they have not deposited themselves. A continuation of these phase-2 efforts is the DoReCo project.[6] DoReCo "brings together spoken lan-

[1] https://aclweb.org/aclwiki/List_of_resources_by_language
[2] https://archive.mpi.nl/tla/
[3] https://elar.soas.ac.uk/
[4] http://www.paradisec.org.au/
[5] http://dobes.mpi.nl/research-projects
[6] http://doreco.info

guage corpora from about 50 languages, extracted from documentations of small and often endangered languages." But for this project, the original corpus creators are typically involved in the creation of an extra layer of annotation. It thus seems fair to say that the existing language archives are currently not available for inspection to researchers outside of the core community of language documenters.[7] Compare this with research on the Switch-Board corpus (Godfrey and Holliman, 1993) or the Penn TreeBank (Marcus et al., 1999), where a lively community has grown around the initial resources and where most researchers are not in direct contact with the initial creators. Looking at possible reasons as to why the uptake of this vast resource of endangered language material is slow, we can come up with an unsurprising set of issues: findability, accessibility, interoperability, and reusability. For a given research question, researchers often need a resource which is a) in a particular format (text, audio, video) b) in a particular language (family) covering c) particular content and is d) accessible. The OLAC[8] (Simons and Bird, 2003) service provides querying capabilities for language and media type, but OLAC cannot guarantee that the resources it lists are indeed available. Since OLAC does not host the files, querying for content strings is not possible either.

A clear desideratum would be the possibility to query language resources based on metadata (region, language format, genre, as currently already possible via OLAC), but also on content. Content includes grammatical categories (give me all files with antipassive in them) but also semantic categories (give me all texts relating to agriculture). This paper will discuss a prototype which allows for such queries. OLAC is already part of the Linked Open Data Cloud (Chiarcos et al., 2012). The task is now to complement the metadata available from OLAC with information about grammatical categories and lexical and topical information which can be extracted from the transcriptions found in the archives. In order to do that, the relevant files have to be retrieved from the archives. An understanding of the structure of these archives is a prerequisite for that.

4. Structure of endangered language archives: *PARADISEC*

Endangered language archives share very similar underlying structures. An *archive* consists of several *collections*. Each collection is about one project, most often covering one particular language, but occasionally, more than one language can be part of a documentation project. A collection in turn consists of *session bundles*, which contain a coherent set of *files* (audio, video, transcription, photos). Files found in a session typically share the same time, location and participants. There can be multiple files of the same type, e.g. very long sessions might have several audio files, with associated transcriptions. The levels of collection, bundle, and file may or may not have their dedicated landing pages, where metadata is displayed. Metadata relevant for a given text is thus often distributed across the various levels. The separation between collections and bundles is not always very clear-cut and is sometimes only available via implicit file naming conventions. The content typically offered consists of audio files, video files, and transcription files. Less common file types include photographs, pdfs, FLEx,[9] Toolbox,[10] praat,[11] and MS Office files. There are typically several levels of access control, which we can enumerate from 1-4:

1. freely available
2. registration and acceptance of terms and conditions required
3. available upon request from depositor
4. unavailable (privacy or other legal issues) (Figure 1, https://catalog.paradisec.org.au/collections/AA1)

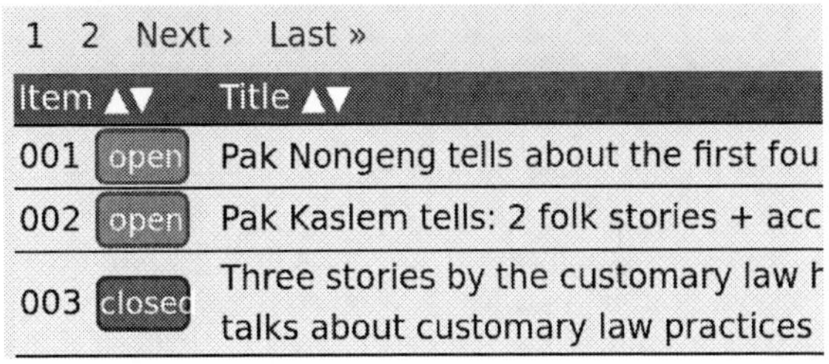

Figure 1: Access levels at PARADISEC.

Turning to findability and reusability, the following picture emerges: The querying possibilities for selected metadata are good. PARADISEC for instance offers nice faceting for country, language, and depositor (Figure 2). Other archives are similar. However, there are no ways to search for a particular language other than scrolling, and the value of metadata fields such as "depositor" or "source university" is not obvious. Other potentially relevant fields are absent from the querying interface, such as "access level" or "media type". I have not been able to formulate a query for "give me a collection which has at least one ELAN file and to which I have access". The only way to perform this query is to visit each and every collection, see whether there are ELAN files and try to download them.

Most archives provide an OAI-PMH[12] interface or have done so in the past.[13] This allows for a uniform query via OLAC.[14] Interestingly, while a query via media type is not possible on the PARADISEC site itself, it is possible on OLAC. The query https://bit.ly/39HueQE returns all sound files for the Namakura language which are available online. Unfortunately, the first bundle listed (*Two Namakura stories*) does indeed contain sound files, but they are not accessible.

Access to linguistic data is a sensitive topic. Next to the domains of privacy and copyright, there are also issues pertaining to language ownership and colonialism, which

[7] The MulitCAST project (https://multicast.aspra.uni-bamberg.de) is similar in setup to DoReCo.

[8] http://search.language-archives.org

[9] https://software.sil.org/fieldworks

[10] https://software.sil.org/toolbox/

[11] http://www.fon.hum.uva.nl/praat/

[12] https://www.openarchives.org/pmh

[13] ANLA and AILLA stopped in 2013 and 2017, respectively, see http://www.language-archives.org/archives

[14] http://search.language-archives.org/index.html

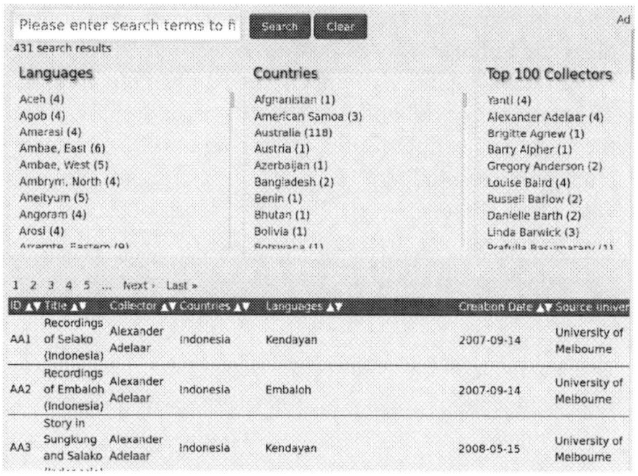

Figure 2: The PARADISEC querying interface.

have different levels of importance in different areas of the world (Holton, 2009). Therefore, archives often have custom terms and conditions, which diverge from better known licensing practices such as Creative Commons. The terms and conditions[15] for the PARADISEC archive for instance include:

> Not to copy the data in whole or in part except insofar as this may be necessary for security purposes or for my own personal use. Not to distribute the data to third parties, nor to publish or reproduce it in any way.
>
> ...
>
> To give access to the data only to persons directly associated with me or working under my control

The language here is very clear: do not copy, do not distribute.

5. The QUEST project

The QUEST (QUality-ESTablished)[16] project has as its stated goal to facilitate the interaction with and mobilization of (endangered) language data via the specification of standards and interfaces. One aspect is the standardization of future input during ingestion, which will facilitate subsequent retrieval. The other aspect is the development of querying tools with uniform interfaces working on extant data. This paper focuses on the latter of these two aspects. To this end, metadata were harvested from OLAC and the five archive websites. All referenced ELAN files were identified and downloaded as far as access restrictions permitted. The resulting set of 20k ELAN files was analysed for internal file structure and a converter into a common backend format was written. A couple of analyses were run on that backend format to prove the viability of the approach. Scripts for harvesting and analysis will be made available together with this paper, but access terms require each researcher collect the data individually from the archives (See §4.).

6. Description of the resources

In the context of this project, data satisfying the following criteria were considered:

1. The data must be programmatically **accessible** via command line tools. Many files in the archives are available "upon request", which means that a formal email has been written to the depositor. This setup does not scale and cannot be handled with the resources currently available. Authentication can be accomplished via the command line so that resources on the "registered user" level could be included.
2. The data must be **interoperable**. For all practical purposes, this means that data has to be in ELAN format.[17] Other file types are found in the archives, but they are either not suitable for data extraction (pdf), or their numbers are too low to justify the time to write an import script.

Current technology does not allow us to search directly in audio (e.g. by humming a melody), let alone in video. This means that querying audio or video boils down to querying transcriptions. The ELAN format is again very suitable, as the text content contained in ELAN is time-linked to multimedia files.

Of the 12 existing DELAMAN archives, 5 were chosen, as they show a variety of setups while at the same time providing a large enough sample of ELAN files to allow for an evaluation of the generic structure of the scripts developed. Table 1 gives a breakdown of the files which could be retrieved from the archives.[18]

ELAN as a file format links audio and video files to transcriptions. Transcription is organised in so-called tiers. Tiers are of a certain type ("translation", "gloss", "POS", etc.) and are hierarchically organised. The hierarchical relation between tiers is typically one of 1) time subdivision (a text is split into time-aligned sentences); 2) symbolic subdivision (a sentence is split into n words, but the words are not time-aligned themselves); and 3) association (a gloss is associated to a word). ELAN can accommodate multiple speakers. These then typically all have their own set of tiers. von Prince and Nordhoff (2020) contain more information about the ELAN file format as used in endangered language projects. Figure 3 shows the XML-representation of an ELAN file. The tier with the TIER_ID "ref@dam" is of the type "ref" and establishes time subdivisions. The tier with the TIER_ID "ut@DAM" references "ref@dam" and is of type "ut" (like 'utterance'). Annotations in tiers of the type "ut" are symbolically associated to the annotations in the parent tier. The tiers of type "ut" have further child tiers, which contain tokenized words ("tx"), morpheme segmentations ("mb") and glosses ("ge"). The tier "ft" contains a free translation for each utterance. Unfortunately for our purposes, the tier types and tier hierarchies are not defined in a specified standard, but are de-

[15] https://catalog.paradisec.org.au/collections/AA1/items/002/essences/967951/show_terms. Apparently, one has to sign in to access the terms and conditions.

[16] https://www.leibniz-zas.de/de/forschung/forschungsbereiche/syntax-lexikon/quest

[17] https://tla.mpi.nl/tools/tla-tools/elan/elan-description

[18] Scripts are available at https://github.com/ZAS-QUEST/eldpy

Table 1: The accessible holdings of the five DELAMAN archives surveyed.

	total		transcriptions			translations	
	files	file size	files	hours	words	files	words
AILLA	2 867	801M	2402	1054:59:29	1 120 059	85	14 284
ANLA	76	14M	48	12:49:40	6 906	45	6 463
ELAR	12 955	3.1G	7189	1470:28:23	1 074 463	706	298 457
PARADISEC	888	167M	706	132:56:03	94 962	153	15 335
TLA	3 473	1 002M	1062	217:20:54	155 476	1 497	72 014

```
<?xml version="1.0" encoding="UTF-8"?>
<ANNOTATION_DOCUMENT>
    <TIME_ORDER>
        <TIME_SLOT TIME_SLOT_ID="ts1" TIME_VALUE="740"/>
        <TIME_SLOT TIME_SLOT_ID="ts2" TIME_VALUE="1860"/>
        <TIME_SLOT TIME_SLOT_ID="ts3" TIME_VALUE="3718"/>
        ...
    </TIME_ORDER>
    <TIER TIER_ID="ref@DAM" PARTICIPANT="Dambar Baram" ANNOTATOR="KP" LINGUISTIC_TYPE_REF="ref">
            <ANNOTATION>
                <ALIGNABLE_ANNOTATION ANNOTATION_ID="ann0" TIME_SLOT_REF1="ts1" TIME_SLOT_REF2="ts2">
                    <ANNOTATION_VALUE>. 001</ANNOTATION_VALUE>
                </ALIGNABLE_ANNOTATION>
            </ANNOTATION>
            <ANNOTATION>
                <ALIGNABLE_ANNOTATION ANNOTATION_ID="ann8" TIME_SLOT_REF1="ts3" TIME_SLOT_REF2="ts4">
                    <ANNOTATION_VALUE>. 002</ANNOTATION_VALUE>
                </ALIGNABLE_ANNOTATION>
            </ANNOTATION>
            ...
    </TIER>
    <TIER TIER_ID="ut@DAM" PARTICIPANT="Dambar Baram" ANNOTATOR="KP" LINGUISTIC_TYPE_REF="ut" PARENT_REF="ref@DAM">
            <ANNOTATION>
                <REF_ANNOTATION ANNOTATION_ID="ann1" ANNOTATION_REF="ann0">
                    <ANNOTATION_VALUE>əbə</ANNOTATION_VALUE>
                </REF_ANNOTATION>
            </ANNOTATION>
            <ANNOTATION>
                <REF_ANNOTATION ANNOTATION_ID="ann9" ANNOTATION_REF="ann8">
                    <ANNOTATION_VALUE>kunəi pudza tukle hon lə məlak</ANNOTATION_VALUE>
                </REF_ANNOTATION>
            </ANNOTATION>
            <ANNOTATION>
                <REF_ANNOTATION ANNOTATION_ID="ann36" ANNOTATION_REF="ann35">
                    <ANNOTATION_VALUE>hidi hudi pudza tukle alam alam wa lakle əbə</ANNOTATION_VALUE>
                </REF_ANNOTATION>
            </ANNOTATION>
            ...
    </TIER>
    <LINGUISTIC_TYPE LINGUISTIC_TYPE_ID="ref"/>
    <LINGUISTIC_TYPE LINGUISTIC_TYPE_ID="ut" CONSTRAINTS="Symbolic_Association"/>
    <LINGUISTIC_TYPE LINGUISTIC_TYPE_ID="txd" CONSTRAINTS="Symbolic_Association"/>
    <LINGUISTIC_TYPE LINGUISTIC_TYPE_ID="tx" CONSTRAINTS="Symbolic_Subdivision"/>
    <LINGUISTIC_TYPE LINGUISTIC_TYPE_ID="mb" CONSTRAINTS="Symbolic_Subdivision"/>
    <LINGUISTIC_TYPE LINGUISTIC_TYPE_ID="ge" CONSTRAINTS="Symbolic_Association"/>
    <LINGUISTIC_TYPE LINGUISTIC_TYPE_ID="ft" CONSTRAINTS="Symbolic_Association"/>
</ANNOTATION_DOCUMENT>
```

Figure 3: The XML structure of ELAN files with tiers referencing each other. Orange lines show references to timeslots, the green line shows the reference to a parent tier, purple shows reference to tier type definitions.

fined on a per-file basis at the very bottom of the XML-file. While ELAN makes sure that annotations are *syntactically* interoperable, *semantic* interoperability is not enforced by ELAN. The tier type containing the translation could be called any of "Translation", "English", "ft" (for free translation), "translation (eng.)" etc. The same goes for transcriptions and glosses. I have compiled a set of all names for tier types (several hundred) and have sorted them into the categories of translation, transcription, gloss, and unknown. This gives some hints about the content in a given tier, but this is not sufficient. The types as indications have to be complemented by information from the tier hierarchy.

The tier hierarchies used in ELAN files are also very heterogeneous. Some files have 3 tiers, some have 4, some have more than 20, and the parent-child relations can be of time subdivision, symbolic subdivision or association. We can establish a fingerprint of the hierarchy via a graph representing the parent-child relations with labelled edges. Table 2 gives an overview of the different configurations found. Among 7 189 ELAN files with transcriptions in ELAR, we find no less than 1 564 different ELAR tier hierarchies. Note that these hierarchies are agnostic of the names given to the tier types; if we included the names, the number would be much higher still.

Finally, some additional tests can be used to ascertain the status of a tier. A tier with English translation should pass

Table 2: Number of different tier hierarchies per archive and the distribution of 7,189 files from ELAR on 1 564 hierarchies.

AILLA	171
ANLA	21
ELAR	1 564
PARADISEC	162
TLA	537

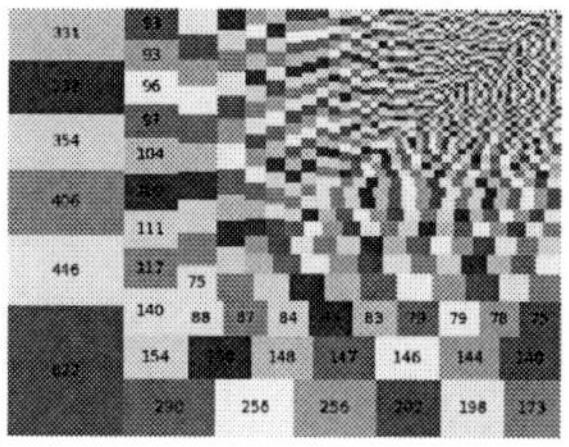

a language detection test for English. A tier with vernacular transcription should fail a language detection test for English. A gloss tier should have close to no white space in its elements; presence of -, = or ALLCAPS words are, on the other hand, good evidence for a tier being a gloss tier and so on.

Based on the names of the tier types, their configurations, and the heuristics/sanity checks just described, we can give the numbers in Table 1 for the accessible holdings of the archives under discussion. The holdings are very different: ELAR has more than two orders of magnitude more available ELAN files than ANLA. and about five times the number of AILLA. But when it comes to transcibed time, AILLA with 1054 hours is not so far behind ELAR with 1470 hours. Apparently, ELAN files hosted at AILLA are more often transcribed than ELAN files at ELAR, which lack retrievable transcriptions in about 40% of the cases. This is reflected in the number of transcribed words, where AILLA with 1.12 million has slightly more than ELAR with 1.07 million, despite having fewer files to begin with. Looking at translations, the picture reverses again: ELAR has now 20 times more translated words than AILLA. The likely interpretation is that for AILLA, transcription is very important, but translation is less of a focus. Compare this to ANLA, where nearly every transcribed file contains a translation. To be fair, many of the projects in AILLA are from Latin America, so that English translations might be absent, but translations in to Spanish or Portuguese might be used instead.

In §3. I mentioned the 67 documentation projects funded by DoBeS. Looking at the 217 hours of transcribed material, this seems very little. Obviously, each of these 67 projects has done more than 3 hours of transcription, and the real amount of transcribed files stored in TLA is much higher. But many of these files are access level 2 (on request) or 3 (unavailable) and are therefore not available for general inspection and analysis. This presents a legal barrier to access. Another reason might be that tier hierarchies or tier type names are very idiosyncratic so that the tiers containing the transcription could not be identified. This would be a technical barrier to interoperability. It is hoped that TLA will address these two barriers to reuse to make sure that the valuable holdings in the "dark repos" can be incorporated into larger research enterprises in the future.

7. Analysis of the resources

Up to now, this article has described the structure of the archives, the structure of ELAN files and the strategies for identifying, retrieving and analyzing ELAN files. In the remainder, I will show some small analyses which can be performed via the uniform access. The analyses presented here have as their main goal the proof-of-concept of a programmatic and uniform access to a large number of ELAN files from diverse locations. They are very simple (even simplistic) on purpose, as the goal here is not to further our understanding of linguistics, but to further our understanding of research infrastructure

7.1. Proof-of-concept: accessing the transcription tier

As a proof of concept, I have computed the most frequent graphemes found in each archive. The plot of the findings is given in Figure 4. The total number of graphemes is 46.5 million. We find, unsurprisingly, that <a> is the most frequent grapheme, and <n> is the most frequent nasal. The order of <e> and <i>, however, is different between archives, suggesting that the languages contained in the respective archives use different orthographies. This is particularly obvious for ANLA, which includes <ł> in the top list.

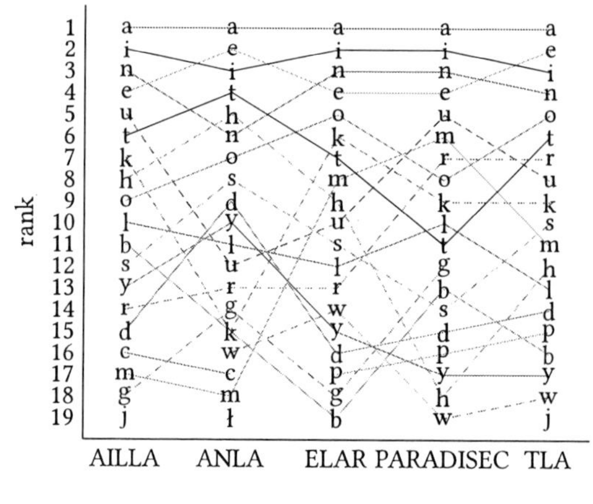

Figure 4: Most frequent graphemes in archives

7.2. Proof-of-concept: accessing the gloss tier

Within the gloss tiers, a total number of 3 274 394 morphemes could be retrieved. Figure 5 gives a breakdown of the most frequent grammatical glosses, while Figure 6 gives a breakdown of the most frequent lexical glosses. ANLA is excluded from both statistics because the amount of gloss material was not sufficient.

Some interesting observations can be made about the most frequent categories here: the number categories singular (SG) and plural (PL) are the most frequent grammatical glosses in ELAR, PARADISEC and TLA. This is not the case for AILLA, where apparently different conventions hold, and P is presumably used for plural instead. This highlights the need for a shared vocabulary, e.g. the Leipzig Glossing

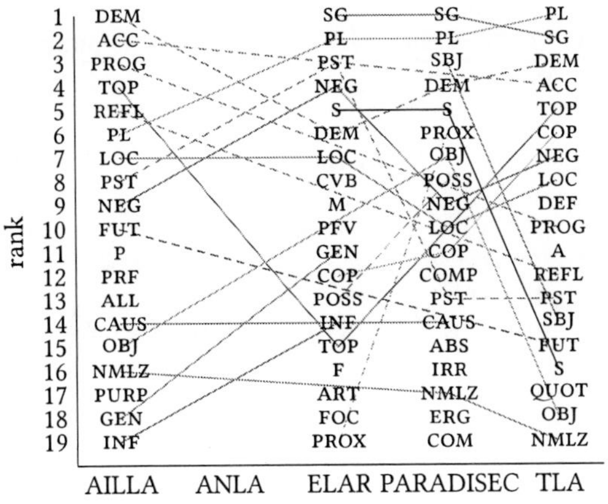

Figure 5: Most frequent grammatical glosses per archive

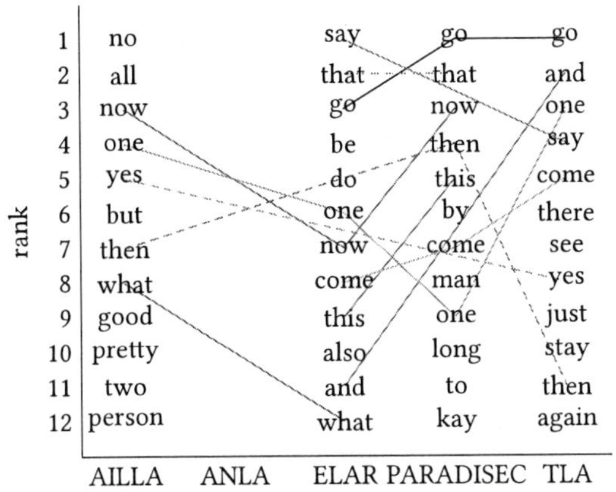

Figure 6: Most frequent lexical glosses per archive

Rules.[19] Another observation is that PST for 'past' is more frequent than FUT for future. This might be due to glossing conventions, the languages observed, or the types of text collected, but it is an interesting observation warranting further inspection.

Another obvious use of these resources would be the extraction of word-gloss-pairs for dictionary bootstrapping, which would be a particular type of text-mining. Table 3 gives words which have been glossed as 'sun' and 'moon' in languages of the corpus, respectively.

These translation data can further be included in a bridge towards Lemon.[20] The full interlinear representation of texts will also be made available in LIGT (Chiarcos and Ionov, 2019) in due course. Data refinements can be achieved with the pyigt library (List and Sims, 2019).

[19]https://www.eva.mpg.de/lingua/resources/glossing-rules.php. The GOLD ontology (Farrar and Langendoen, 2003) is often cited in this context, but has failed to develop any big impact due to a number of conceptual problems.

Table 3: Strings glossed as 'sun' and 'moon' in the corpus, which can be used for dictionary bootstrapping.

sun	moon
ane; eelo; hiisiis; hɛ; iisiis; indi;	biikousiis;
koyaš; künɣaraɣï; lainta; lezha;	bulan; cəlauni;
lénjí; lo'aa; mijiri; mə̃13;	din; goe-; hi; ilu;
mə̃13læ31; mə̃13lɛ33; mə̃31;	kàru; luna; lɔ13;
mə̃31la31; mə̃31læ31; mə̃33;	maham; moon;
mə̃33læ55; mə̃35; mə̃55; niel;	mɨŋgramɨn;
p'ûûs; siβu; siβun; siβuŋ; sool; sun;	owniv; o:lɛ:;
sunə; tèle; tse/imá; tʰa55ia53; uni;	sahr; t'aar; turu;
vala'; was; yaal; yal; yaro; ³tini;	tún; wula; ōl;
âftâw; čeli; ŋar; şımş; ŋɔ13; ʔawá	ɔ́tɔ̀'

7.3. Proof-of-concept: accessing the translation tier

The proof-of-concept for the extraction of the translations from an ELAN tier involves Named Entity recognition via the NERD/GROBID online service.[21] Table 4 gives a breakdown of the entities retrieved. Tables 5 and 6 show the most frequent entities retrieved and the entities retrieved exactly 20 times. Taking a look at the concepts retrieved, we find a strong focus on agriculture, and on the Svan people from Georgia. The latter is a clear indication that the corpus is skewed and that there is an exceedingly large amount of well-transcribed files from a documentation project in the Caucasus, from where entities could easily be retrieved. But while this shows that one cannot simply run a quantitative analysis on the archives and be done, it also shows that the very high quality of the Caucasian data make the data much more findable and interoperable, giving them automatically a greater weight in scientific knowledge production. The "Caucasus bias" is obvious from the data, but at the same time, the "agriculture bias" is also something to take into account. Apparently, documentation projects more often focus on rural communities and crops/livestock than on urban settings and technology for instance. This must be borne in mind when drawing conclusions from the files stored in endangered language archives.

NERD/GROBID returns a Wikidata-ID (Vrandečić and Krötzsch, 2014), which allows to include the endangered language data in the wider Linked Open Data Cloud. This can be leveraged for semantic queries of the sort "give me all texts with a passive in them which deal with crops". For this query, we do not have to query for "maize", "rice", "wheat", "millet", etc. since Wikidata stores the in-

[20]https://lemon-model.net/

[21]http://cloud.science-miner.com/nerd

Table 4: Entities retrieved from DELAMAN archives.

	total entities	different entities
AILLA	1 532	592
ANLA	301	142
ELAR	20 991	6 091
PARADISEC	1 163	568
TLA	10 346	3 281

Table 5: Most frequent retrieved entities across all archives.

#	Wikidata-ID	meaning
537	Q830	cattle
281	Q144	dog
271	Q11575	maize
270	Q7368	domestic sheep
250	Q5090	rice
239	Q383126	chronic condition
230	Q34067	Svan
212	Q5113	bird
209	Q2934	goat
204	Q19044	Svaneti
204	Q1364	fruit
187	Q626136	Arapaho people
184	Q8495	milk
184	Q532	village
177	Q190	God
166	Q7802	bread
163	Q13187	*Cocos nucifera* (coconut)
159	Q43238	*Poaceae* (grass)
158	Q503	banana
154	Q10798	pig
146	Q670887	*Bambusoideae* (bamboos)
145	Q11254	table salt
144	Q10998	potato
131	Q127980	fat
129	Q35808	firewood
120	Q846578	Svan people
117	Q1029907	stomach
115	Q10943	cheese
113	Q780	chicken
113	Q35409	family
101	Q41415	soup

formation all of these concepts are subclasses of https://www.wikidata.org/wiki/Q12117 "cereal", which in turn is subsubclass of https://www.wikidata.org/wiki/Q235352 "crop". Wikidata can furthermore be utilized for localization of queries: The data available about the concept https://www.wikidata.org/wiki/Q5090 "rice" contain translations into 171 languages, among which we find the translation into Swahili, *wali*. A constantly resurfacing requirement for archive mobilization is the accessibility to the speaker communities themselves. Being able to accept queries in a local language of wider communication, such as Swahili, is a crucial step for making the data *about* an ethnic group also being usable *by* that ethnic group.

8. Discussion

I have surveyed the existing language archives, and I have shown how a large corpus of ELAN files can be retrieved from these archives. These ELAN files are amenable to programmatic access, allowing to aggregate transcriptions, translations, and glosses, which can then be further analysed with regard to graphemes, grammatical categories or semantic fields. Two strands of research can be distinguished here. The first one is linguistics proper ("Which

Table 6: Some medium frequency retrieved entities

#	Wikidata-ID	meaning
20	Q102192	freshwater
20	Q103459	livestock
20	Q107434	Sioux
20	Q11995	human pregnancy
20	Q125525	jackal
20	Q159334	secondary school
20	Q164088	*Metroxylon sagu* (sago palm)
20	Q184418	coffin
20	Q193110	floodplain
20	Q39861	*Hirundinidae* (swallows)
20	Q41692	mule
20	Q42302	clay
20	Q6450151	Kwande (district in Nigeria)
20	Q7632586	success

categories are used?"). The other one is closer to the sociology of science ("Which categories are used in which archives, and why? Which archives have more transcriptions, which ones have more translations, and why?"). Linguistics is often seen as a science bridging the gap between the natural sciences and the humanities. The first strand mentioned above is closer to the empirical approach, while the second strand is more a question typically asked within the humanities. The language resource assembled here can be used for both.

For purely quantitative research, the resource is obviously not suitable in its current state, as the "Caucasian bias" discussed in §7.3. shows. But a parametrization taking into account collections, languages, or even language families via genealogical data available from Glottolog is reasonably trivial.

But what can we do with the data? As mentioned above in §4., the ELAN files themselves cannot be shared due to the terms of access. In a linked data context (Chiarcos et al., 2012), however, this is not necessary. Once we have proper URIs which resolve to a given resource, we can use these as variables in our predicates. We can say that https://catalog.paradisec.org.au/collections/DLGP1/items/053 is a session which is about `glottolog:nama1268`, the URI for Namakura on Glottolog. We can say that a given session includes a file, which includes a tier, which includes a gloss which is the same as one of the Leipzig Glossing Rules glosses. The structures of the archives with collections, bundles, and files were discussed in §4.. In a linked data context, each collection, bundle, and file should have a different URI, but not all archives provide landing pages for all of those (Simons and Bird, 2020). Things get more difficult when using tiers or their parts (annotations) in Linked Data predicates, as the tiers and annotation will have to get URIs as well. A good solution for a resolver service will have to be developed, which will allow the use of these elements in assertions without requiring read or write access to the archives where the primary resources are hosted. This resolver will also help make the data findable by being citable, with exact location of the element in question in archive, collection, file, and tier. Using such a resolver service will also allow the incorporation of sensitive data into the Linguistic Linked Open Data Cloud. We can say that the session with a given URI contains information about human sexual activity (https://www.wikidata.org/wiki/Q608), but we do not have to provide the session itself. This has obvious use cases in linguistics, but also in related fields of the humanities, such as anthropology or musicology. In the field of material culture, for instance, anthropologists look at items and appliances produced and used by given groups. Depending on the nature of the research question, broader or narrower concepts will be appropriate. In the domain of boat building, some researcher might be interested in all seafaring vessels, while for another one, only boats, only canoes, or only dugouts are relevant. A well-defined and ontologically grounded vocabulary for material culture can help the formulation of sensitive queries then (see e.g. eHRAF[22]).

What we can share, however, are download scripts for harvesting the archives. These scripts can be run by third party researchers and will provide the same files we have on our computers, but the third party researchers themselves have to agree to the terms and conditions before the download.

Interested researchers can request access from the relevant archive. Using Wikidata as a "semantic broker" also helps discoverability via the different language labels provided for the concepts, as described in §7.3..[23]

9. Outlook

Nordhoff et al. (2016) describe the Alaskan Athabascan Grammar Database (AAGD), which is also concerned with the findability of resources for endangered languages. For that project, texts from a number of native Alaskan languages were collected and made retrievable via a SOLR store. This SOLR store allowed faceted searches for metadata, but also for content categories such as semantic concepts and grammatical categories contained. While background and technology used are different, the requirements for the AAGD and this project are very similar. At the time of writing, the main focus is still the data model and the backend, but the repurposing of some of the frontend materials from the AAGD project should not be too difficult. The next step ahead will be the adaptation of the AAGD frontend to the QUEST datamodel. This adaptation will also allow for an easy integration of a "recommendation system". Such as system can use the texts a researcher has stated their interest in and propose new transcribed texts based on similarity in grammatical or semantic categories contained.

The main challenge ahead is the minting of URIs which adequately identify collections, sessions, files and tiers. This must be complemented by a useful ontology. Dublin Core isPartOf is used as an umbrella term for the time being, but more explicit relations would be useful.

Another technical challenge is the realization of federated queries. We need information from OLAC, Glottolog, Wikidata, and our own QUEST data. Ideally, OLAC as a central hub should provide the content searches described in this paper next to the metadata searches. If this is not to happen, a choice must be made whether one wants to go for some federated structure,[24] or whether a new service should be set up, which will periodically be updated with dumps from the other knowledge bases.

10. Acknowledgements

This research is funded by the German BMBF, as part of the QUEST project. I would like to thank Frank Seifart, Felix Kopecky, Hanna Hedeland, Mandana Seyfeddinipur, Kilu von Prince, and two anonymous reviewers for comments on previous versions of this paper.

11. Bibliographical References

Chiarcos, C. and Ionov, M. (2019). Ligt: An LLOD-Native Vocabulary for Representing Interlinear Glossed Text as RDF. In Maria Eskevich, et al., editors, *2nd Conference on Language, Data and Knowledge (LDK 2019)*, volume 70 of *OpenAccess Series in Informatics (OASIcs)*, pages 3:1–3:15, Dagstuhl, Germany. Schloss Dagstuhl–Leibniz-Zentrum fuer Informatik.

Chiarcos, C., Hellmann, S., and Nordhoff, S. (2012). Linking linguistic resources: Examples from the Open Linguistics Working Group. In Christian Chiarcos, et al., editors, *Linked Data in Linguistics. Representing Language Data and Metadata*, pages 201–216. Springer, Heidelberg.

Farrar, S. and Langendoen, D. T. (2003). A linguistic ontology for the semantic web. *GLOT International*, 7(3):97–100.

Holton, G. (2009). Relatively ethical: A comparison of linguistic research paradigms in Alaska and Indonesia. *Language Documentation & Conservation*, pages 161–175.

List, J.-M. and Sims, N. A. (2019). Towards a sustainable handling of inter-linear-glossed text in language documentation. Preprint under review. Not peer-reviewed.

Nordhoff, S., Tuttle, S., and Lovick, O. (2016). The Alaskan Athabascan Grammar Database. In Nicoletta Calzolari (Conference Chair), et al., editors, *Proceedings of the Tenth International Conference on Language Resources and Evaluation (LREC 2016)*, Paris, France, may. European Language Resources Association (ELRA).

Simons, G. F. and Bird, S. (2020). Expressing language resource metadata as linked data: The case of the open language archives community. In Antonio Pareja-Lora, et al., editors, *Development of Linguistic Linked Open Data Resources for Collaborative Data-Intensive Research in the Language Sciences*. MIT Press, Cambridge.

von Prince, K. and Nordhoff, S. (2020). An empirical evaluation of annotation practices in corpora from language documentation. In *Proceedings of LREC 2020*. Marseille.

[22]https://ehrafworldcultures.yale.edu

[23]Providing labels in different languages is a first step towards interculturally adequate discoverability. Wikidata itself probably has a significant Western bias in the selection and organisation of the concepts it contains. This bias cannot be resolved here.

[24]For instance in the context of CLARIN Federated Content Search architecture.

12. Language Resource References

Godfrey, J. J. and Holliman, E. (1993). *Switchboard-1 Release 2 LDC97S62.* Linguistic Data Consortium, Philadelphia.

Harald Hammarström, et al., editors. (2019). *Glottolog 4.0.* Max Planck Institute for the Science of Human History, Jena.

Marcus, M. P., Santorini, B., Marcinkiewicz, M. A., and Taylor, A. (1999). *Treebank-3 LDC99T42.* Linguistic Data Consortium, Philadelphia.

Simons, G. and Bird, S. (2003). The Open Language Archives Community: An infrastructure for distributed archiving of language resources. *CoRR*, cs.CL/0306040.

Vrandečić, D. and Krötzsch, M. (2014). Wikidata: A free collaborative knowledgebase. *Commun. ACM*, 57(10):78–85.

Proceedings of LR4SSHOC: Workshop about Language Resources for the SSH Cloud, pages 19–26
Language Resources and Evaluation Conference (LREC 2020), Marseille, 11–16 May 2020

Verbal Aggression as an Indicator of Xenophobic Attitudes in Greek Twitter during and after the Financial Crisis

Maria Pontiki, Maria Gavriilidou, Dimitris Gkoumas, Stelios Piperidis
Institute for Language and Speech Processing (ILSP), ATHENA Research and Innovation Center
Artemidos 6 & Epidavrou, 15125, Marousi, Greece
{mpontiki, maria, dgkoumas, spip}@athenarc.gr

Abstract

We present a replication of a data-driven and linguistically inspired Verbal Aggression analysis framework that was designed to examine Twitter verbal attacks against predefined target groups of interest as an indicator of xenophobic attitudes during the financial crisis in Greece, in particular during the period 2013-2016. The research goal in this paper is to re-examine Verbal Aggression as an indicator of xenophobic attitudes in Greek Twitter three years later, in order to trace possible changes regarding the main targets, the types and the content of the verbal attacks against the same targets in the post crisis era, given also the ongoing refugee crisis and the political landscape in Greece as it was shaped after the elections in 2019. The results indicate an interesting rearrangement of the main targets of the verbal attacks, while the content and the types of the attacks provide valuable insights about the way these targets are being framed as compared to the respective dominant perceptions and stereotypes about them during the period 2013-2016.

Keywords: Verbal Aggression, Xenophobia, Twitter

1. Introduction

Xenophobia is broadly defined as intense dislike, hatred or fear of those perceived to be strangers (Master and Roy, 2000). As a psychological state of hostility or fear towards outsiders (Reynolds and Vine, 1987), xenophobia is associated with feelings of dominance (implying superiority) or vulnerability (implying the perception of threat), respectively (Veer, 2013). As a disposition, xenophobia can be the basis of racism, fascism, and nationalism (Delanty and O'Mahony, 2002), since it is often rooted in (cultural, religious, racial, etc.) prejudices or driven by ideology.

Focusing mainly on the effects and the consequences of xenophobia in social life -rather than its conceptual formulation- Delanty and O'Mahony (2002) describe it as *rooted in the symbolic violence of everyday life*, while Bronwyn (2002) suggests that xenophobia is more than just an attitude towards foreigners; it can also take shape as a practice, and in particular as a violent practice. In this context, Verbal Aggression (VA) constitutes an important component in the study of xenophobia; aggressive messages targeting foreigners can be indicative of xenophobic attitudes. VA involves using messages to attack other people or those aspects of their lives that are extensions of their identity (Hamilton and Hample, 2011). The forms of aggression are manifold and vary from expressions of disgust and contempt, to threats, slander, insults, and hatred (Rösner and Krämer, 2016). The close relation of online VA with xenophobia is also demonstrated by the hate speech literature and especially by approaches that focus on xenophobia-related types of hate speech like racist (Kwok and Wang, 2013; Waseem and Hovy, 2016) and hate speech directed to immigrants (Sanguinetti et al., 2018) or to specific ethnic groups (Warner and Hirschberg, 2012), even though no explicit reference to xenophobia is made.

Traditionally, xenophobia is measured using data coming from focus groups, interviews, and public sentiment polls using standard questions in order to capture opinions, emotions, perceptions and beliefs (e.g. Eurobarometer). Despite the numerous research efforts in automatically detecting and analyzing online sentiment, VA and hate speech, user-generated content has been scarcely explored from the xenophobia measuring perspective in a large scale. A major up-to-date research effort that examined xenophobia as a violent practice using computational social science and big data techniques is the XENO@GR project[1]. Based on the research hypothesis that xenophobia is a deeply rooted social phenomenon that reasonably escalates under circumstances of severe economic crisis, the project aimed to examine whether (or not) xenophobia in Greece is an outcome of the financial crisis or it comprises a long-lasting social perception deeply rooted in the Greek society. This research puzzle was decomposed into specific Research Questions (RQs) and xenophobia was examined in terms of physical aggression (event analysis) and verbal aggression (VA) towards specific Target Groups, as attested in two types of textual data, namely news and tweets, using data mining techniques. Focusing on VA, almost 4.5 million Tweets covering the period 2013-2016 were analyzed using a VA analysis framework that provided valuable insights regarding the main targets and types of the verbal attacks, and the main stereotypes and prejudices about the TGs of interest during the financial crisis, helping the political and social scientists to formulate adequate responses to the project's RQs (Pontiki, 2019; Pontiki, Papanikolaou, and Papageorgiou, 2018).

In this paper we present a replication of the VA analysis framework three years later; in 2019 Greece is in the post financial crisis era, but the refugee crisis is still ongoing. In addition, the centre-right party New Democracy has won the 2019 general election ousting the left-wing Prime Minister Alexis Tsipras, while Golden Dawn -a neo-Nazi party that evolved from a marginal group into Greece's third-largest party during the financial crisis- was knocked out of the Parliament, as a result of the last elections. The research goal is to examine if the VA analysis framework can trace any imprint of these changes on public beliefs

[1] Project Website: http://xenophobia.ilsp.gr/?lang=en

and attitudes expressed in Twitter about the specific TGs; the results indicate an interesting rearrangement of the main targets of the verbal attacks, while the content and the types of the attacks provide valuable insights regarding how these TGs are being framed as compared to the respective dominant stereotypes about them during the period 2013-2016.

The remainder of this paper is structured as follows. Section 2 provides an overview of the methodology and the VA analysis framework that was used for both periods. The results for the period 2013-2016 and for the year 2019 are presented in Sections 3 and 4, respectively. The paper concludes with a discussion on the main findings (Section 5), as well as on the contribution and the limitations of the proposed methodology (Section 6).

2. Methodology

This paper focuses on VA analysis; event analysis is not discussed here. The current section elaborates on the methodology applied for the analysis of Twitter data, aiming at the identification of verbal attacks against specific target groups. This methodology was designed initially in the framework of XENO@GR project and applied on data from the period 2013-2016 and subsequently re-applied on 2019 Twitter data, in order to examine possible shifts in xenophobic reactions in the country in the post-crisis era. Results of the first experiment are presented in Section 3 while results from the second experiment in Section 4.

Xenophobia is a complex social phenomenon that reflects a deep-rooted form of fear and hostility towards the other, who is perceived as a stranger to the group oneself belongs to. In the context of the XENO@GR project the notion of other was limited to people with other than Greek nationality or origin, and further restricted to the following ten predefined TGs of interest based on specific criteria (e.g. population of the specific ethnic groups in Greece, dominant prejudices in Greece about the specific groups): TG1: PAKISTANI, TG2: ALBANIANS, TG3: ROMANIANS, TG4: SYRIANS, TG5: MUSLIMS/ISLAM, TG6: JEWS, TG7: GERMANS, TG8: ROMA, TG9: IMMIGRANTS, TG0: REFUGEES. IMMIGRANTS and REFUGEES were considered as two generic TGs and examined separately due to the different connotations and implicatures of these two lexicalizations; the research hypothesis was that people framed as *immigrants* are more likely to receive xenophobic behaviors rather than those framed as *refugees*. In addition, there are legal protection differences between *immigrants* and *refugees*; refugees are specifically defined and protected by international law, particularly regarding refoulement.

The overall workflow for building the framework was a five-step process, including the creation of textual and lexical languages resources and Natural Language Processing (NLP) tools for their processing. Specifically: **A. Data Collection.** For each TG of interest relevant Tweets were retrieved using related queries/keywords e.g. *ισλάμ* (Islam). The search function in the database configuration was stemmed, so the queries returned also Tweets containing morphological variations of the selected keywords. A total of 4.490.572 Tweets was retrieved covering the period 2013-2016. Fig. 1 illustrates the per-year amount of Tweets for each TG. **B. Data Exploration.** Samples of the collected data were manually explored in order to identify different aspects of VA related to the predefined targets of interest. **C. Knowledge Representation.** Based on data observations and literature review findings, a linguistically-driven typology of VA messages was designed (2.1). **D. Computational Analysis.** The data was modelled using the appropriate resources and algorithms that were designed and implemented for the computational treatment of the VA framework (2.2). **E. Data Visualization.** The output, having been revised, was visualized in various ways making the analysis results explorable, comprehensible and interpretable with regard to the RQs under study.

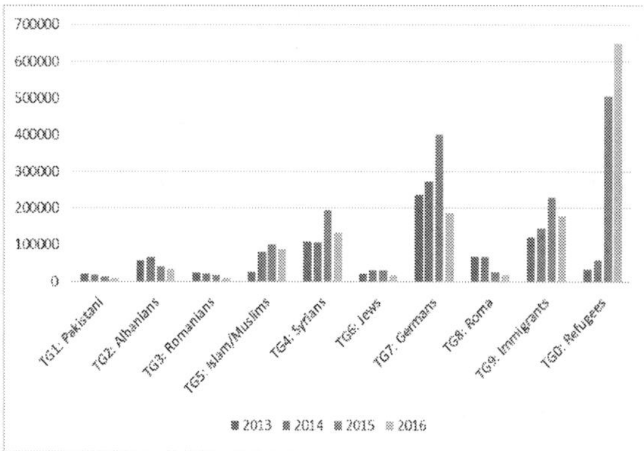

Figure 1: Amount of collected Tweets per year and TG.

2.1 Typology of VA Messages

Based on literature review and explorative analysis findings a linguistically-driven framework was developed where VA messages (VAMs) are classified based on: (a) their focus (distinguishing between utterances focusing on the target's attributes, and utterances focusing on the attacker's thoughts), (b) the type of linguistic weapon used for the attack, and (c) the content of the attack (e.g. threats/calls for physical violence or for deportation). The detailed typology is illustrated in Fig. 2 (Pontiki, 2019; Pontiki, Papanikolaou, and Papageorgiou, 2018).

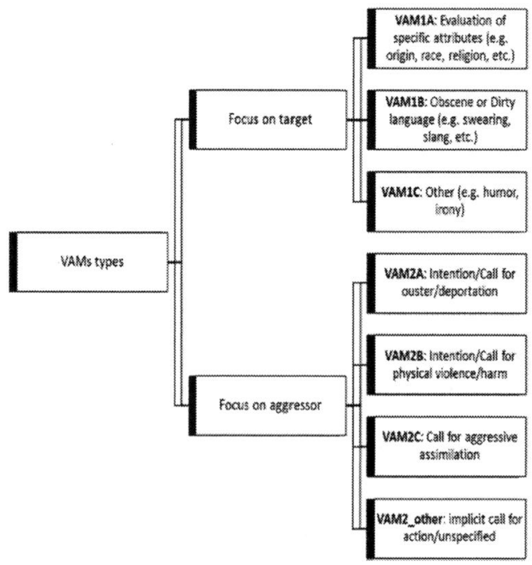

Figure 2: Typology of VAMs.

As illustrated above, two main types of VAMs are considered and further categorized in specific subtypes. (I) **VAM1.** Messages focusing on (the attributes of) the target (e.g. physical appearance, religion, etc.) further classified into subcategories based on the type of the linguistic devices (weapons) used by the aggressor to attack the target: formal evaluations of specific attributes (VAM1A), taboo or dirty language (VAM1B), and more complex linguistic devices such as humor or irony (VAM1C). (II) **VAM2.** Messages focusing on the aggressor's intentions providing information about specific types of attacks further classified into subcategories based on the content of the attack: intentions or calls for ouster/deportation -oriented to legal means- (VAM2A), intentions or calls for physical violence/harm -oriented to physical extinction- (VAM2B), calls for aggressive assimilation (VAM2C), and implicit or unspecified calls for action (VAM2D).

The typology was designed to provide both quantitative and qualitative information about the verbal attacks enabling to interpret VA as an indicator of xenophobic attitudes by addressing specific RQs based on the amount (main targets of the attacks), the type and the content (stereotypes and prejudices) of the aggressive messages.

2.2 VA Computational Framework

For the computational treatment of the above typology a linguistically-driven VA analyzer was designed. The approach is lexicon-based and explores shallow syntactic relations between aggressive terms (i.e. words that are used to express VA) and sequences of tokens-candidate targets of the attacks. The input is raw data. First, the data is processed through a NLP pipeline that performs tokenization, sentence splitting, part-of-speech tagging, and lemmatization using the ILSP suite of NLP tools for Greek (Papageorgiou et al., 2002; Prokopidis, Georgantopoulos and Papageorgiou, 2011), available through the CLARIN:EL infrastructure (https://www.clarin.gr/en), (Piperidis, Labropoulou, and Gavrilidou, 2017). Then, the analyzer detects candidate VAMs and targets based on the respective lexical resources. Finally, sets of grammars/ linguistic patterns determine which spotted candidate VAMs and targets are correct and classify them according to the typology.

The method is precision-oriented and focuses on explicitly stated VA; it relies on a set of lexical resources built to capture possible linguistic instantiations of VA towards the TGs of interest. VAMs that are instantiated through complex linguistic structures and devices (i.e. humor, implicit calls for action), and cannot be captured at the lexical level were considered out of scope. Exceptions were some specific cases of VAM1C and VAM2D that were found repeatedly in the data -reproducing some well-known stereotypes towards specific TGs- and were addressed using lexico-syntactic patterns. The performance of the VA analyzer was evaluated using a random selection of 500 Tweets per TG (5000 Tweets in total) in terms of Precision (84%), Recall (60%) and F-Measure (68%). Evaluation was performed also separately for each TG-specific sub-collection in order to obtain a more fine-grained and in-depth view of the results. More details about the VA framework and the experimental evaluation can be found in (Pontiki, 2019).

3. VA Analysis Findings for 2013-2016

The collected data (Fig.1) was processed using the VA analyzer. The output was recorded in a Knowledge Database (KD) and was, subsequently, used for statistical analysis and visualizations. For each processed Tweet, the KD was populated with two types of information: **A.** Annotations derived by the automatic VA analysis: TG_id (e.g. TG5), TG_evidence (the lexicalization of the TG as referred to in the Tweet e.g. *Ισλάμ* (Islam)), VAM_type (e.g. VAM1A), and VA_evidence (the lexicalization of the verbal attack as it appears in the Tweet e.g. *σκοταδισμός* (obscurantism)), and **B.** Twitter metadata: timestamp, User_id, and the Tweet text. A summary of the main findings with regard to the RQs under study is presented in the following sections.

3.1 Main Targets of Verbal Attacks

As illustrated above in Fig. 1, the most discussed TGs during 2013-2016 were REFUGEES and GERMANS. The peak in the mentions of REFUGEES during 2015-2016 coincides with the refugee crisis in Europe, whilst GERMANS were continuously in the limelight since, along with the IMF and the EU, the German Government had a central role in the Greek crisis. The next most discussed TGs were IMMIGRANTS and SYRIANS -also related with the refugee crisis-, and MUSLIMS/ISLAM, with a peak from 2014 onward which coincides with the rise of ISIS. However the number of Twitter mentions is not necessarily indicative of the amount of the verbal attacks against each TG. The VA analysis results (Fig. 3) indicate that the most mentioned TGs are not always the most attacked ones as well (e.g. REFUGEES were the most discussed but the least attacked TG).

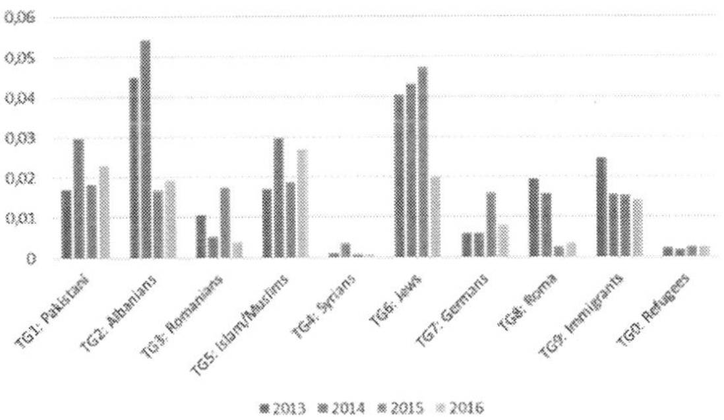

Figure 3: Per-year VA rate (VAMs/Tweets) per TG.

The most attacked TGs were JEWS, ALBANIANS, PAKISTANI, MUSLIMS/ISLAM, and IMMIGRANTS. Antisemitism appeared to be at the core of xenophobic discourse. This finding is in par with the findings of the ADL Global 100[2] survey, according to which Greece was the most anti-Semitic country in Europe -based on the strength of anti-Semitic stereotypes- scoring 69%. The role of anti-Semitism in the Greek political culture during that period had attracted attention after a series of opinion poll findings and most importantly after the rise of neo-Nazi Golden Dawn, a party with an explicit anti-Semitic discourse (Georgiadou, 2015).

[2] http://global100.adl.org/public/ADL-Global-100-Executive-Summary.pdf

ALBANIANS are perhaps the most established group of foreigners in Greek public discourse, given that the image of foreigner as it was constructed in Greece during and after the first wave of migration flow (early-mid 1990s) was mainly associated with Balkan -and mainly- Albanian nationality (Voulgaris et al., 1995). As for the generic group IMMIGRANTS, the results confirmed that it is more likely to verbally attack groups of people framed as IMMIGRANTS rather than as REFUGEES probably due to the different connotations/implicatures of these two lexicalizations. MUSLIMS have a long presence in Greece[3], however, the verbal attacks that targeted them were triggered by geopolitical events such as the rise of ISIS or events related to violent practices or sexual abuse of specific population groups (women, children). The information about the types and the content of attacks presented below provides interesting insights helping to better comprehend and interpret these findings.

3.2 Main Types of Verbal Attacks

The overall number of messages that express VA focusing on the target of the attack (VAM1) was quite bigger than the number of messages focusing on the aggressor's intentions (VAM2); the proportion of the detected VAMs of type 1 and 2 was approximately 89% and 11%, respectively. Focusing on VAM1 attacks, the TGs who were mostly attacked with messages negatively evaluating specific attributes of theirs (VAM1A) were ALBANIANS and JEWS, whilst PAKISTANI and IMMIGRANTS received the most obscene messages (VAM1B).

Focusing on VAM2 attacks, JEWS received most of them with ALBANIANS and PAKISTANI following in the second and third place, respectively (Fig. 8). In fact, calls for physical extinction (VAM2B) were much more for JEWS than for any other group. What needs to be noted is that there is not a significant number of JEWS living in Greece as compared to ALBANIANS and PAKISTANI that constitute the largest immigrant populations in this country. Moreover, aggressive messages related to JEWS reveal the emergence of threat perception based on biological and cultural terms, as well as the perception of a particular enmity towards the Greek nation (see also below 3.3). Threat perception seems to prevail also for PAKISTANI, ALBANIANS and IMMIGRANTS, according to the share of VAM2 attacks and, in particular, the calls for ouster/deportation (VAM2A) for the specific groups.

3.3 Stereotypes and Prejudices

Stereotypes and prejudices were examined focusing on the content of the verbal attacks. To this end, the linguistic evidence of the aggressive messages was visualized using word clouds containing the unique aggressive terms found per TG, based on the assumption that the unique linguistic weapons used against each TG may be associated with specific types of attributes or themes discussed per TG. The qualitative analysis of the results confirmed the existence of stereotypes and prejudices against specific TGs that are deeply rooted in Greek society. In the case of JEWS, the verbal attacks entailed a perception of a particular enmity towards the Greek nation and blame attribution patterns of the Greek crisis. As illustrated in Fig. 4, *εχθρότητα* (hostility) was the most frequent term tagging them. Common themes in this group of messages were the identification with the negative aspects of the banking system and global capitalism, as well as the frequent appeal to conspiracy theory elements e.g. *δολοπλόκος* (conniver), *διπλοπροσωπία* (double-faced), *καιροσκόπος* (opportunist), while Greece and banks were often tagged as *Εβραιοκρατούμενη* (owned by Jews). These findings are in par with the conclusions drawn from the survey of Antoniou et al. (2014) who established a correlation between conspiratorial thinking and ethnocentricism, and elaborated an interpretation of Greek anti-Semitism building on aspects of national identity and by employing the concept of victimhood. Another deeply rooted stereotype in Greek society that was reflected also in the verbal attacks against JEWS is the perception that they are avaricious e.g. *φραγκοφονιάς* (cheeseparing). Anti-Semitic attitudes entailed also notions of hate-speech e.g. the use of the term *σαπούνι* (soap) in a biting derogatory manner referring to soap made of Jewish victims by the Nazis.

Figure 4: Word Cloud of unique aggressive terms for JEWS.

A perception of a particular enmity towards the Greek nation was also dominant in the verbal attacks against GERMANS, who played a central role in the Greek crisis. The popularity of the anti-German attitudes in Greece was also attested by a series of public opinion findings (Pew Global Attitudes Project, 2012[4]). In the case of Twitter, a variety of evaluative terms were used to stress out the harshness and hostility of GERMANS against Greeks. Memories and symbols of WWII and of Nazi occupation of Greece were also instrumentalized in the context of this victimization repertoire. These findings suggested a resurgence of the anti-German narration in the context of the anti-austerity (anti-memorandum) discourse. Anti-German narration is considered to be the most prominent formulation of a victimization repertoire based on the foreign enemy concept and on the limited sovereignty discourse (Lialiouti and Bithymitris 2013).

The verbal attacks in the case of ALBANIANS and PAKISTANI entailed different perceptions; the dominant stereotypes in the construction of the image of ALBANIANS were associated with *crime* and *cultural inferiority* indicating a continuity of the so-called stereotype of the Balkanian criminal. The inferiority stereotype was also dominant for PAKISTANI; with the exception of some

[3] The Muslim minority in Thrace is the only officially recognized minority in Greece.

[4] https://www.pewresearch.org/global/2012/12/12/social-networking-popular-across-globe/pew-global-attitudes-project-technology-report-final-december-12-2012/

messages focusing on poor personal hygiene, physical appearance or the color of skin, PAKISTANI were mostly evaluated as inferior beings with derogatory morphological variations of their nationality name as a linguistic weapon. Crime and inferiority stereotypes were dominant also in the case of MUSLIMS/ISLAM, but with rather different aspects; the attacks were often lexicalized through evaluative and dysphemistic terms of insult or abuse to debase core Islamic values, practices, etc. indicating irrationalism, sexist behavior and fanaticism.

3.4 Discussion and Further Insights

The VA analysis framework designed in the context of the XENO@GR project provided valuable insights regarding the main targets and types of the verbal attacks, and the main stereotypes and prejudices about the TGs of interest during 2013-2016 helping the political and social scientists to address the project's RQs. According to these findings, xenophobia in Greece, when examined in terms of Twitter VA towards specific TGs of interest, seems to be culturally-rooted and not crisis-driven. The qualitative analysis of the aggressive messages argues in favor of a continuity of deeply rooted stereotypes about specific TGs (e.g. ALBANIANS, JEWS). However, the results indicate also the emergence of attacks that are associated with blame attribution patterns about the Greek crisis (e.g. GERMANS, JEWS). In other words, xenophobic attitudes may not be crisis-driven, but the economic crisis encourages the development of defensive nationalism and the perception of vulnerability. As for the refugee crisis that was in its peak during 2015-2016, its effect on public beliefs remained an open question for future research. The few verbal attacks that were captured against REFUGEES were mostly attempts to challenge their identity implying that they are illegal immigrants. This notion of illegality or lawlessness was also dominant in the case of IMMIGRANTS, who were mostly framed as *λαθρομετανάστες* and *λάθρο* (illegal).

The results illuminate also two different dimensions correlated to the conceptualization of xenophobia. On the one hand, attacks against TGs who are considered powerful (JEWS, GERMANS) are related to the concept of vulnerability, implying the perception of threat. As for the perception of vulnerability related to MUSLIMS/ISLAM, the attacks that entailed notions of Islamophobia were mostly triggered by the rise of ISIS and did not seem to constitute a core component of the Greek xenophobia, at least at that time period. On the other hand, dominance is directed against TGs thought of as inferior in socio-economic or cultural perspectives (ALBANIANS, PAKISTANI).

4. VA Analysis Findings for 2019

Following the same methodology as for the period 2013-2016, we retrieved relevant Tweets for each TG of interest. The search resulted in ten collections, which contain a total of 1.672.783 Tweets and cover the time period from 1/01/2019 until 31/12/2019. As it is illustrated in Fig. 5, REFUGEES, IMMIGRANTS, and SYRIANS continue to be in the limelight due to the ongoing refugee crisis. GERMANS, also remain a highly mentioned TG. The Tweets were processed with the same VA analysis framework used for the period 2013-2016.

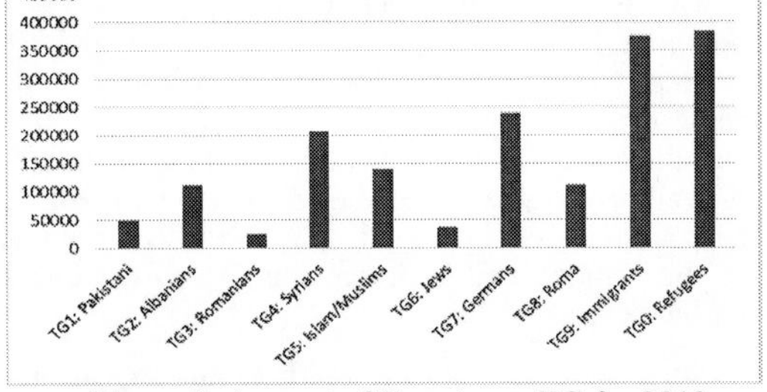

Figure 5: Amount of Tweets per TG for 2019.

4.1 Main Targets of Verbal Attacks

Fig. 6 illustrates the VA rate per TG for both periods enabling a direct comparison of the mostly attacked TGs during and after the financial crisis. Overall, the quantitative analysis of the verbal attacks indicates that xenophobic behaviors do not seem to be so dominant in Greek Twitter, since the VA rates (VAMs/Tweets) regarding the specific TGs in both periods are low (i.e. the VA rate for the mostly attacked TG is approx. 5%). Focusing on 2019, according to the results, the main targets are the same 5 TGs (JEWS, ALBANIANS, PAKISTANI, IMMIGRANTS and MUSLIMS/ISLAM) but they appear in different positions on the list. In particular, we observe an interesting shift of the two mostly attacked TGs during 2013-2016 (JEWS and ALBANIANS), to the 5th and 4th place, respectively, in 2019, and a respective elevation of PAKISTANI, IMMIGRANTS and MUSLIMS/ISLAM as the top three attacked TGs.

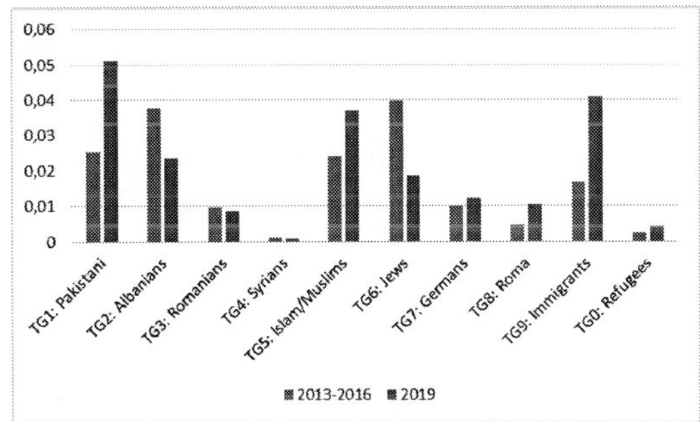

Figure 6: VA rate per TG and time period.

The fact that JEWS do not constitute the main target of the verbal attacks in the post crisis era seems to validate the findings during the crisis period; beside the culturally-rooted stereotypes, the verbal attacks against them entailed also blame attribution patterns about the Greek crisis and frequent appeal to conspiracy theory elements in the context of defensive nationalism and a perception of vulnerability. So, it could be argued that in the post crisis era, with the lessening of the feeling of vulnerability towards JEWS, the focus has been shifted to other groups who afflict the Greek society (PAKISTANI, IMMIGRANTS). This argument is also supported by the qualitative analysis of the content of the attacks (4.3).

Another important element that has to be taken into account in the interpretation of these results, is the weakening of the main source of anti-semitic discourse in Greece; the neo-Nazi party Golden Dawn has been framed as a criminal organization with its leadership being accused of a number of violations and put on a long-running trial for the murder of an anti-fascist activist. Furthermore, other extreme rightwing politicians -no Golden Dawn members- who used to generate an explicit anti-semitic discourse during the crisis, are now members of the center-right government, and thus actively involved in the country's relations with Israel (e.g. the trilateral cooperation among Israel, Greece and Cyprus to build a natural gas subsea pipeline).

The decreased rate of the verbal attacks against ALBANIANS can be possibly examined in relation to the increased one against PAKISTANI; the third generation of ALBANIANS that came in Greece during the first migration flow is more or less integrated in the Greek society, while many of them have started going back to Albania. On the other hand, the migration flow from Asia is more recent. In addition, the term PAKISTANI, and especially its derogatory morphological variations, seems to be used as a generic term framing migrants that came to Greece from other Asian countries as well (e.g. Afghanistan, Bangladesh, Iraq) and not only from Pakistan.

The increased rate of the attacks against IMMIGRANTS can be possibly attributed to the ongoing refugee crisis and mainly to the fact that the effect of this crisis has started to be tangible in the Greek society, especially at the severely overcrowded camps on the islands (e.g. Moria in Lesvos). As for the REFUGEES, the results confirm again that it is more likely to verbally attack groups of people framed as IMMIGRANTS rather than as REFUGEES.

4.2 Main Types of Verbal Attacks

Fig. 7 illustrates the VAM1A/B rates for the five mostly attacked TGs for both periods enabling a direct comparison between them. As it is indicated by the share of the VAM1B rates, in 2019 IMMIGRANTS receive more attacks of this type than PAKISTANI as compared to the period 2013-2016, but still these two TGs constitute the main recipients of obscene messages in both periods. The rearrangement of the main targets of the attacks described in the previous section is reflected in the share of the VAM1A rates; the TGs who are mostly attacked with messages negatively evaluating specific attributes of them in 2019 appear to be MUSLIMS/ISLAM and PAKISTANI, and not JEWS and ALBANIANS as in 2013-2016.

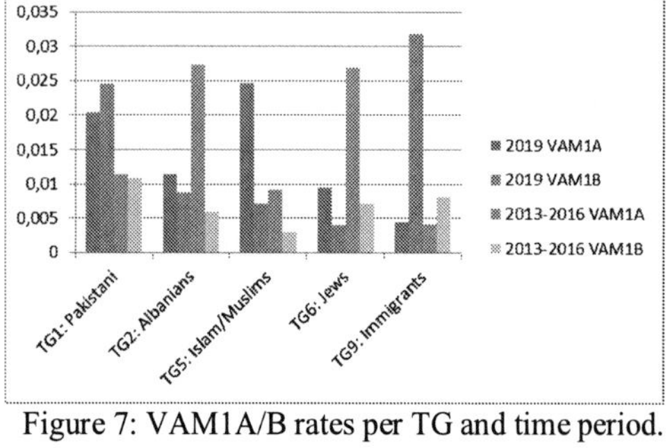

Figure 7: VAM1A/B rates per TG and time period.

JEWS may not constitute the main target of formal evaluations expressed in Twitter after the crisis, however, as it is illustrated in Fig. 8, they remain the main recipients of VAM2 messages and especially of calls for physical distinction; taking also into account that there is not a significant number of JEWS living in Greece as compared to the population of other groups in Greece (PAKISTANI, ALBANIANS, IMMIGRANTS), anti-semitism seems to still constitute a core component of the Greek xenophobia in the post crisis era. Another interesting finding is the increase of the VAM2 messages, in particular of the calls for ouster/deportation, against MUSLIMS/ISLAM; taking also into account the respective increase of such calls against PAKISTANI and IMMIGRANTS, this finding could indicate a possible interconnection between these three TGs.

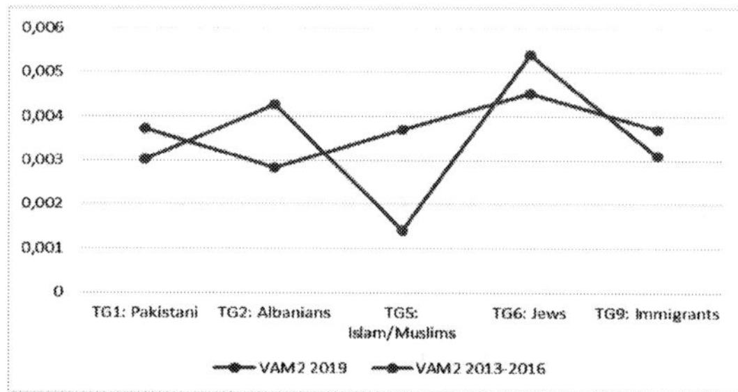

Figure 8: VAM2 rates per TG and time period.

4.3 Stereotypes and Prejudices

The qualitative analysis of the content of the attacks provides interesting insights regarding the dominant stereotypes and prejudices about the TGs under study also in the post crisis era. In the case of JEWS, the verbal attacks against them still entail a perception of a particular enmity towards the Greek nation and notions of hate-speech; the main terms in the construction of their image remain *εχθρότητα* (hostility) and *σαπούνι* (soap). However, as it is indicated in Fig. 9, the decrease of the rate of the attacks against them in 2019 is reflected also in the summary of the unique aggressive terms used to frame them as compared to the respective one in 2013-2016 (Fig. 4). Another interesting observation is the weakening of the "avarice" stereotype, which is a deep-rooted perception about JEWS in Greek society. Along with the financial crisis also the blame attribution patterns are also gone, while Greece and banks are no longer tagged as owned by Jews. The absence of the blame attribution patterns about the Greek crisis is observed also in the attacks against GERMANS.

Figure 9: Word Cloud of unique aggressive terms for JEWS.

In the case of ALBANIANS and PAKISTANI, the content of the verbal attacks captured against them in 2019 does not portray any major differences as compared to the attacks against them in the period 2013-2016; with the exception of a relative weakening of the criminality stereotype for ALBANIANS, they both keep being framed as inferior beings mainly through derogatory morphological variations of their nationality name (*Αλβανά*, *Πακιστανά*). No major differences arise also in the case of

MUSLIMS/ISLAM; the stereotypes that are derived by the semantics of the unique aggressive terms for the particular TG in 2019 are the same as in 2013-2016 (i.e. fanaticism, cultural inferiority, brutal violence, sexism, and irrationalism). As for IMMIGRANTS, the most frequent terms used to frame them in both time periods are the words *λαθρομετανάστες* (illegal immigrants) and *λάθρο* (slang term for illegal). Given the generic nature of this TG, in that they do not constitute specific ethnic group with individual characteristics, no unique aggressive terms about them were found. In both periods they are generally evaluated as inferior beings mainly in terms of cultural inferiority, criminality, and poor personal hygiene.

5. Discussion

We presented a replication of the VA analysis framework that was designed in the context of the XENO@GR project aiming to examine VA as an indicator of xenophobic attitudes in Twitter during the financial crisis in Greece, in particular during 2013-2016. The research goal of this paper was to re-examine VA as an indicator of xenophobic attitudes in Greek Twitter three years later, in the post crisis era, using the same NLP pipeline and lexical resources on a new dataset. The aim was to trace possible changes regarding the main targets, the types and the content of the verbal attacks against the same TGs, given also the ongoing refugee crisis and the political landscape in Greece as it was shaped after the elections in 2019. The results indicate an interesting rearrangement of the main targets of the verbal attacks; the two mostly attacked TGs during 2013-2016 (JEWS and ALBANIANS) are shifted to the 5th and 4th place, respectively, while PAKISTANI, IMMIGRANTS and MUSLIMS/ISLAM appear to be the top three attacked TGs in 2019.

The subsidence of the verbal attacks against JEWS seems to be in accordance with the remission of the financial crisis as well as with the switchover of the political landscape in Greece in 2019; verbal attacks against them are fewer and do not convey blaming for the crisis as in the period 2013-2016. Anti-semitic discourse in Greece has lost its main representative, the neo-Nazi party Golden Dawn. However, the types and the content of the attacks once again indicate anti-semitism as a core component of the Greek xenophobia confirming the existence of dominant perceptions that are deeply rooted in the Greek society and keep being reproduced after the financial crisis.

The increased rate of the verbal attacks against IMMIGRANTS seems to coincide with the ongoing refugee crisis; as a main entry point for asylum seekers and migration in Europe, Greece is still struggling to cope with the migration flows, while the effect of this crisis is now tangible, especially at the severely overcrowded camps on the islands. The types and the content of the attacks against them indicate that IMMIGRANTS are mainly framed as illegal, inferior and unwelcome, as in the period 2013-2016.

In the case of MUSLIMS/ISLAM, the results indicate an increase of islamophobia notions as compared to the period 2013-2016; the stereotypes that are derived by the semantics of the unique aggressive terms for the particular TG in 2019 are the same as in 2013-2016. However, the increase of the calls for deportation of MUSLIMS/ISLAM in 2019, taking also into account the respective increase of such calls against PAKISTANI and IMMIGRANTS, may indicate a qualitative difference as compared to 2013-2016, when the verbal attacks against MUSLIMS/ISLAM were mostly triggered by geopolitical events such as the rise of ISIS; this finding could indicate a possible interconnection between these three TGs and remains an open question for future research.

ALBANIANS and PAKISTANI constitute the largest immigrant populations in Greece. ALBANIANS are perhaps the most established group of foreigners in Greek public discourse, since the first wave of migration flow (early 1990s-mid 1990s). Almost thirty years later, and although they are more or less integrated in the Greek society, while many of them have started going back to Albania, they still are a main target of xenophobic attitudes. On the other hand, the migration flow from Asia is more recent. In addition, the content of the verbal attacks suggests that the term PAKISTANI -especially its derogatory morphological variations - seems to be used as a generic term framing migrants from other Asian countries as well (e.g. Afghanistan, Bangladesh, Iraq) and not only from Pakistan. A possible reconstruction of the image of foreigner in Greece that seems to be indicated by these findings remains an open question for future research.

6. Limitations and Contribution

Xenophobia is a complex social phenomenon that reflects a deeply rooted form of fear and hostility towards the "other", who is perceived as a stranger to the group oneself belongs to. In the work presented in this paper, the notion of "other" is restricted to ten predefined TGs of interest based on specific criteria. Xenophobia is examined as a violent practice in terms of VA that constitutes only one aspect of xenophobic attitudes. Hence, the findings of this work provide insights in the context of a specific case study and not for the phenomenon of xenophobia in Greece in general. Furthermore, the findings result from Social Media data, in particular from a single platform study (snapshots of the Greek Twitter), hence they are not representative of the demographics and the attitudes of the general population in Greece.

In this setting, the work presented in this paper constitutes an example of how a language technology-based method can serve as a complementary research instrument in the context of Social Sciences and Humanities. Taking a step further from typical computational approaches, this work linked the results (the output of the method) to specific RQs including the critical step of their interpretation and presented an interdisciplinary end-to-end approach. The VA analysis framework was designed to provide both quantitative and qualitative information about the verbal attacks, helping to study the formulation of VA in relation to specific TGs, and to measure and monitor different aspects of VA as an important component of the manifestations of xenophobia in Greek Twitter.

The proposed framework can be extended to other targets (e.g. homophobic cyber-attacks) as well as to other languages, enabling cross-country studies and cross-cultural comparisons. Furthermore, given the high correlation between verbal and physical aggression (Hamilton and Hample, 2011) -in that VA may escalate to physical violence-, and the fact that physical and verbal attacks in the context of the XENO@GR project seem to be addressed to the same targets (Pontiki, Papanikolaou, and Papageorgiou, 2018), the proposed framework could provide valuable insights not only to political and social scientists but also to other stakeholders (e.g. policy makers).

7. Acknowledgements

The authors are grateful to Prof. Vasiliki Georgiadou, Professor of Political Science the Panteion University of Social and Political Sciences, for her valuable contribution in the interpretation of the results, and to Dr. Dimitris Galanis, Researcher at ILSP/ATHENA, for his help in the data processing phase. The work presented in this paper is supported by the Social Sciences & Humanities Open Cloud (SSHOC) project (https://www.sshopencloud.eu/) funded by the EU framework programme Horizon 2020 and APOLLONIS, the National Infrastructure for the Digital Humanities and Sciences and Language Technology and Innovation, project (https://apollonis-infrastructure.gr/), MIS 5002738, funded by the Operational Programme Competitiveness, Entrepreneurship and Innovation 2014-2020 (EPAnEK).

8. References

Antoniou, G., Dinas, E., Kosmidis, S. and Saltiel, L. (2014). *Antisemitism in Greece: Evidence from a Representative Survey.*

Bronwyn, H. (2002). A new pathology for a new South Africa? In D. Hook and G. Eagle (Eds), *Psychopathology and Social Prejudice* (pp. 169–184), Cape Town: University of Cape Town Press.

Delanty, G. and OMahony, P. (2002). *Nationalism and social theory: Modernity and recalcitrance of the Nation.* London: Sage.

Georgiadou, V. (2015). *Antisemitism in Greece: Concerns and considerations.* In: Antisemitism in Greece. Athens: British Embassy.

Hamilton, M. and Hample, D. (2011). Testing Hierarchical Models of Argumentativeness and Verbal Aggressiveness. *Communication Methods and Measures*, 5(3), pp. 250–273.

Kwok, I. and Wang, Y. (2013). Locate the hate: Detecting tweets against blacks. In: *Proceedings of the 27th AAAI Conference on Artificial Intelligence (AAAI 2013)*, Bellevue, Washington, 14-18 July, 2013, pp. 1621–1622.

Lialiouti, Z. and Bithymitris, G. (2013). The Nazis Strike Again': the concept of 'the German Enemy', party strategies and mass perceptions through the prism of the Greek economic crisis. In Karner, C. and Mertens, B. (Eds.) *The Use and Abuse of Memory: Interpreting World War II in Contemporary European Politics* (pp. 155–172). New Brunswick & London: Transaction Publishers.

Master, S. D. and Roy, M. K. (2000). Xenophobia and the European Union. *Comparative Politics*, 32 (4), pp. 419–436.

Papageorgiou, H., Prokopidis, P., Demiros, I., Giouli, V., Konstantinidis, A., and Piperidis S. (2002). Multi–level XML–based Corpus Annotation. In: *Proceedings of the 3rd International Conference on Language Resources and Evaluation (LREC 2002)*, Las Palmas, Spain, pp. 1723–1728.

Piperidis, S., Labropoulou, P. and Gavrilidou, M. (2017). clarin:el: a language resources documentation, sharing and processing infrastructure [in Greek]. In Georgakopoulos, T., Pavlidou, T.-S.,Pehlivanos, M. et al (eds), Proceedings of the 12th International Conference on Greek Linguistics, pp. 851–869. Berlin: Edition Romiosini/CeMoG.

Pontiki, M. (2019). Fine-grained Sentiment Analysis. PhD Thesis. University of Crete. [Online] Available at: http://thesis.ekt.gr/thesisBookReader/id/46115#page/1/mode/2up

Pontiki, M., Papanikolaou, K. and Papageorgiou, H. (2018). Exploring the Predominant Targets of Xenophobia-motivated behavior: A longitudinal study for Greece. In: *Proceedings of the 11th International Conference on Language Resources and Evaluation (LREC 2018), Natural Language Meets Journalism Workshop III*, Miyazaki, Japan, pp. 11 –15.

Prokopidis, P., Georgantopoulos, B., and Papageorgiou, H. (2011). A suite of NLP tools for Greek. In: *Proceedings of the 10th International Conference of Greek Linguistics*, Komotini, Greece, pp. 373–383.

Reynolds, V. and Vine, I. (1987). *The sociobiology of ethnocentrism: Evolutionary dimensions of xenophobia, discrimination, racism and nationalism.* London: Croom Helm.

Rösner, L., and Krämer, N. C. (2016). Verbal Venting in the Social Web: Effects of Anonymity and Group Norms on Aggressive Language Use in Online Comments. *Social Media & Society*, 2(3), pp. 69–94.

Sanguinetti, M., Poletto, F., Bosco, C., Patti, V. and Stranisci, M. (2018). An Italian Twitter Corpus of Hate Speech against Immigrants. In: *Proceedings of the 11th International Conference on Language Resources and Evaluation (LREC-2018)*, Miyazaki, Japan, pp. 2798–2805.

Strötgen, J. and Gertz, M. (2012). Temporal tagging on different domains: Challenges, strategies, and gold standards. In Calzolari et al. (eds), Proceedings of the 8th International Conference on Language Resources and Evaluation (LREC'12), pp. 3746–3753, Istanbul, Turkey.

Veer, K. V., Ommundsen, R., Yakushko, O., Higler, L., Woelders, S. and Hagen, K. A. (2013). Psychometrically and qualitatively validating a cross-national cumulative measure of fear-based xenophobia. *Quality & Quantity,* 47(3), pp. 1429–1444.

Voulgaris, Y., Dodos, D., Kafetzis, P., Lyrintzis, C., Michalopoulou, K., Nikolakopoulos, E. and Tsoukalas, K. (1995). Perceiving and dealing with the Other in present day Greece. *Elliniki Epitheorissi Politikis Epistimis,* 5, pp. 81–100.

Warner, W and Hirschberg, J. (2012). Detecting hate speech on the World Wide Web. In: *Proceedings of the 2012 Workshop on Language in Social Media (LSM 2012)*, Montreal, Canada, 7 June, 2012, pp. 19–26.

Waseem, Z. and Hovy, D. (2016). Hateful Symbols or Hateful People? Predictive Features for Hate Speech Detection on Twitter. In: *Proceedings of the NAACL 2016 Student Research Workshop*, San Diego, California, 13-15 June, 2016, pp. 88–93.

Proceedings of LR4SSHOC: Workshop about Language Resources for the SSH Cloud, pages 27–32
Language Resources and Evaluation Conference (LREC 2020), Marseille, 11–16 May 2020

Mining Wages in Nineteenth-Century Job Advertisements
The Application of Language Resources and Language Technology to study Economic and Social Inequality

Ruben Ros,[1] Marieke van Erp,[2] Auke Rijpma,[1,3] Richard Zijdeman[3,4]
[1]Utrecht University
[2]KNAW Humanities Cluster DHLab
[3]International Institute for Social History
The Netherlands
[4] University of Stirling
Scotland
r.s.ros@uu.nl, marieke.van.erp@dh.huc.knaw.nl,
a.rijpma@uu.nl, richard.zijdeman@iisg.nl

Abstract

For the analysis of historical wage development, no structured data is available. Job advertisements, as found in newspapers can provide insights into what different types of jobs paid, but require language technology to structure in a format conducive to quantitative analysis. In this paper, we report on our experiments to mine wages from 19th century newspaper advertisements and detail the challenges that need to be overcome to perform a socio-economic analysis of textual data sources.

Keywords: historical newspaper, job ads, occupations, income analysis, information extraction

1. Introduction

Economists and sociologists draw on historical data to study long term trends. Information from archival records is used, for example to assess intergenerational mobility (Knigge, 2016). Overall, relative to contemporary data, historical quantitative data are hard to come by, and seldom the result of a research oriented data gathering process. As a result, researchers have to deal with what is available: a signature to indicate someone's literacy, relative height to proxy health and the rounding of numbers ('age heaping') as an indicator of a population's numeracy. In that sense even occupation is a proxy for a person's human, economic and social capital.

Historians draw, next to quantitative sources, on qualitative sources. For example, by manually studying 617 memoirs for reasons why people put their children too work, or rather try to keep from work (Humphries, 2003). Another example is (Schulz et al., 2014) who painstakingly derived ascribed and achieved characteristics from 2194 job employment advertisements. However, compared to the derivation of occupational information, mining such qualitative data is even more labour intensive and will therefore always lead to relatively small samples, reducing the statistical power of hypothesis tests.

In this paper, we expand on these sources by using a computer assisted method, text mining, to extract from a qualitative source an occupation specific characteristic: wage. Wages are one of the most important long-run data series being gathered. They are a headline measure of long-run living standards and economic leadership (Allen, 2001; Allen et al., 2011; Feinstein, 1998; de Zwart et al., 2014). The Malthusian view of pre-industrial societies being characterised by long-term income stagnation relies on wages and prices for its empirical support (Clark, 2005). Furthermore, wage data are a key component in current explanations for the timing and location of industrialisation and the transition to sustained growth (Allen, 2009).

However, there has been substantial criticism at the methodology used in such research. Daily wages from a narrow set of occupations (construction workers) are made comparable through a standardised CPI and working days estimate. The degree to which such estimates are representative over all occupations and the places for which we have wages, as well as the assumptions about hours worked are increasingly criticised as biasing results (Stephenson, 2018; Humphries and Schneider, 2019; Humphries and Weisdorf, 2019). Overall, the call is to broaden the horizon in the type of sources being used to obtain historical wage data.

In this paper, we present a text mining use case for the social science and humanities domain. We describe a rule-based classifier that is used on a large corpus of job advertisements to analyse the development of wages. With this approach, we can automatically extract wages from a wide range of occupations and places. We describe our experiments and results, as well as the challenges in working on non-digital born resources and with a corpus that displays diachronic language variation.

The remainder of this paper is organized as follows. In the next section, we describe related work followed by the data sources used in Section 3. We then describe our approach in processing and analysing the wage information from digitized newspapers in Section 4. Our evaluation is presented in Section 5. followed by our conclusions and future work in Section 7. The code used in this project, as well as the lists of occupation titles and qualitative wage indicators can be found on: `https://github.com/rubenros1795/mining-job-ads`

2. Related work

To the best of our knowledge, advertisements have only occasionally been used in historical sociology and economic history. Schulz et al. use job advertisements to study whether people are hired for their ascribed or achieved characteristics (Schulz et al., 2014). Gray also collects quantitative data from newspaper advertisements, in this case rental prices to study the New York rental market (Gray, 2018). However, so far all these studies rely on manual entry to extract information from advertisements. One exception is Cummins, who uses regular expressions to extract information on wealth at death from the printed volumes of the Principal Probate Registry of the United Kingdom between 1892–2016 (Cummins, 2019). Automating this process further, and evaluating the results systematically, can greatly increase the usability of this kind of source material.

Automatically extracting information from text is a well-developed task in natural language processing research (Weischedel and Boschee, 2018). However, occupations are not a category of concepts that are generally included in such tasks, which often focus on named entities and relations between them. Many such approaches are based on machine learning methods, but annotating training data for this work was out of the scope of our project. Furthermore, the non-digital born nature of the source material used in our study also affects the quality of automatic methods (van Strien et al., 2020).

3. Data

The Dutch National Library has undertaken several large-scale digitization projects, resulting in a collection of over 15 million pages of digitized newspapers spanning the period between 1618 and 1995.[1] Newspapers printed before 1876 are free of copyright restrictions. For the post-1876 newspapers, access was granted by the National Library. Besides the text of the newspaper articles (made machine-readable with Optical Character Recognition), various metadata fields such as dates, newspaper titles and links to the original images are also available.

The Dutch National Library has assigned four categories to different newspaper articles: news, advertisements, personal announcement, and illustrations. This makes it relatively straightforward to extract advertisements. For this project, we focused on advertisements in all newspapers present in the National Library database printed between 1850 and 1890. Although newspaper advertisements appear as early as the seventeenth century, it was only the mid-nineteenth century that saw the rise of large-scale newspapers, structured in a relatively consistent way and including relatively stable categories of advertisements.

After downloading the advertisements, they were preprocessed by removing all non-alphanumeric characters, followed by lowercasing and tokenization. We decided not to lemmatize the corpus because we suspected that the low OCR quality of the ads would hinder proper lemmatization. The statistics of the (preprocessed) data are summarized in Table 1. We measure OCR quality using the type-token ratio (TTR), which is the relative number of unique words divided by the relative number of words. Because faulty OCR produces many non-existent words, it is expected that texts with a low OCR-quality have a relatively high number

[1]https://delpher.nl

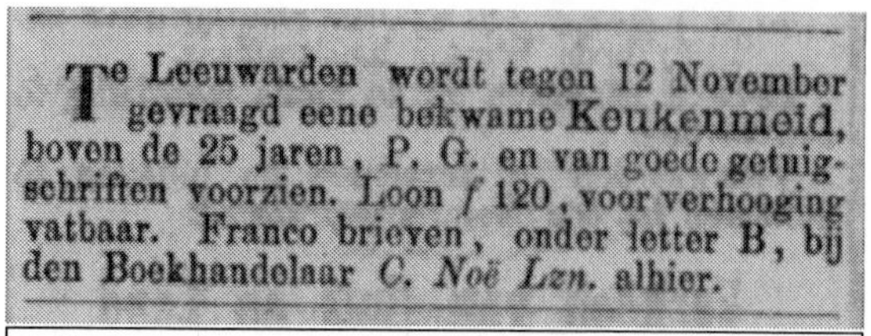
Te Leeuwarden wordt tegen 12 November gevraagd eene bekwame Keukenmeid, boven de 25 jaren, P. G. en van goede getuigschriften voorzien. Loon f 120, voor verhooging vatbaar. Franco brieven, onder letter B, bij den Boekhandelaar C. Noë Lzn. alhier.

rpo Leeuwarden wordt tegon 12 November I gevraagd eene bekwamo Keukenmeid, boven de 25 jaren, I. O. en van goedo getuigschriften voorzien. Loon / 120, voor verhooging vatbaar. Franco brieven, onder letter B, bij den Bockhandolaar C. Nof Len. alhier.

In Leeuwarden is by 12 November asked one skilled kitchen maid, over 25 years old, P. G. and with good reference letters. Salary f120, increase possible. Post paid letters, under letter B. at the Bockshop C. Noë. Lzn. in this town.

Figure 1: Example of a non-preprocessed job advertisement in *Leeuwarder Courant* (19-7-1878) and its translation in *italics*

of unique words (types). The ratio between the number of words and the number of unique words in a given year thus forms an approximation of OCR quality. Since a higher number of articles often leads to a higher number of types we divide both the number of tokens and the number of types by the number of articles.

According to (Reynaert, 2008), a TTR of around 44% is expected for twentieth-century newspapers. Wevers reports type-token ratios between 5% and 25% in the period 1890-1910 (Wevers, 2017). The quality of the OCR in the ads used in this study is quite low, especially compared to similar measurements in earlier studies. The low scores for the material used in this study are likely to result from the visual complexity of advertisements (compared to news articles). This also explains the decline in type-token ratios in the period between 1850 and 1879. In this period, an increase in the number of advertisements and the growing size of newspaper pages led to more complex page compositions that are harder to process for OCR engines.

Figure 1 shows an example of a job advertisement published in 1878. The photographed newspaper is provided, as well as the translation in *italics*. OCR errors are marked in red.

4. Approach

The approach to extract information from job advertisements consists of two tasks. First, the job advertisements (currently not labelled as such by the National Library) need to be identified from the overall set of advertisements. The second step is to extract "wage indicators" from the advertisements and connect them to specific occupations.

4.1. Extracting Job Advertisements

Because a single advertisement (identified as such by article segmentation metadata provided by the National Library) often contains multiple advertisements (Figure 2) we need to detect potentially multiple occupations and associated wages per article. Especially job advertisements are

	1850-1859	1860-1869	1870-1879	1880-1889
pages	1,491,391	3,321,334	3,534,270	3,427,923
articles	303,631	562,584	645,721	525,792
tokens	$1,1E+08$	$1,7E+08$	$1,72E+08$	$1,35E+08$
types	6,048,407	10,344,452	13,227,808	10,233,301
TTR	18%	16%	13%	13%

Table 1: Description of the dataset: the number of pages, the total number of articles, the total number of tokens, the total number of types and the type token ratio (TTR). The TTR is calculated as the ratio between the relative number of tokens (words) and the relative number of types (unique words).

sensitive to poor segmentation because they are generally short and do not have a consistent visual appearance. From all the advertisements that contain occupation titles, around 80% contain multiple titles. This problem could be solved by implementing a new segmentation procedure or by training a classifier to find relevant segments within the overall text, but this was out of the scope of this project.

ORNAMENTEN.
De Ondergeteekende berigt door deze, dat hij een zeer groot MAGAZIJN heeft opgerigt VAN ALLE SOORTEN VAN
KUNST-ORNAMENT,
hetwelk uitmunt door zijne luchtigheid en nette bewerking.
Hij vleit zich door de zoo groote verscheidenheid ruimschoots aan een ieders keuze te kunnen voldoen. Dit Magazijn is van HEDEN, dagelijks voor een ieder te bezigtigen bij den Ondergeteekende, welke hetzelve beleefdelijk aanbeveelt, belovende in alles daarop betrekking hebbende, eene uiterst civiele en propere bediening.
Schiedam, M. H. ENGERING, Sz.,
Februarij 1854. (1196) Mr. Metselaar, Stukadoor, enz.

Edinburgh Ale, London Porter en Dublin Stout,
te bekomen bij JAMES GIBSON, Herderstraat, te Rotterdam. (9251)

TREKPLEISTER VAN ALBESPEYRES VOOR FONTANELLEN.
36 jaren geneeskundig succes in Frankrijk en in den vreemde, bewijzen de voortreffelijkheid der TREKPLEISTERS VAN ALBESPEYRES. 1°. Blaartrekkend-Linnen, om de Fontanellen aan te leggen, binnen weinige uren, zonder Pleisters. 2°. Papier van Albespeyres, om alleen het overvloedig en gelijkmatig Etteren te onderhouden, zonder reuk of pijn. 3°. Verzachtend Papier, voor de volledige verbinding der Fontanellen, waarvan het de ontsteking en de jeukte weert, enz. enz. 4°. Pommade van Albespeyres, om de Fontanel-Erwten en de Ettering aan den gang te houden. Verkrijgbaar bij de meeste Apothekers; te Rotterdam bij VAN SANTEN KOLFF. Men gelieve te letten op het cachet en de handteekening van den Uitvinder ALBESPEYRES, om schadelijke en gevaarlijke namaaksels te vermijden. (8043)

WORMKOEKJES
van Fr. BRABENDER, Apotheker en Chemiker in Cleve.
Ik verklaar gaarne, dat de door den Heer BRABENDER vervaardigde Wormkoekjes uit onschadelijke Wormverdrijvende middelen en zuivere Chocolade bestaan, en door mij sedert een jaar wel in honderd gevallen, zonder eenig nadeel voor de Patienten, met zeer goed gevolg gebruikt zijn. Behalve hunne zekere werking zijn ze aanbevelenswaardig, omdat zij door de Kinderen, waar toch de wormen het meest voorkomen, zoo gaarne genomen en

Op een Commissie Kantoor alhier, wordt gevraagd
EEN BEDIENDE,
eenigzins bekend met het EXPEDITIE VAK en CONVOOILOOPERS WERK, en de Hoogduitsche taal niet onkundig.
Hierop reflecterenden gelieven zich franco te adresseeren, met eigenhandig geschreven brieven, onder letter IJ, bij de Boekverkoopers M. WIJT & ZONEN. (1272)

Er wordt te 's Gravenhage met primo Mei a. s. gevraagd in een Koffij- en Theewinkel, eene
WINKELDOCHTER,
tusschen de 25 en 35 jaren oud en van de Prot. Godsdienst. Aanvragen eigenhandig, schriftelijk en gefrankeerd, onder letter B, aan de Boekhandelaars A. VAN HOOGSTRATEN en ZOON, te 's Gravenhage. (1239)

Voor MEID ALLEEN,
wordt gevraagd eene ordelijke DIENSTBODE, van de R. C. Godsdienst, om dadelijk in dienst te treden.
Adres: Binneweg, 15—371. (1256)

Tegen Mei aanst. wordt verlangd eene Bekwame
KEUKENMEID,
van de P. G., tegen Zeventig Gulden Huur.
Te bevragen bij den Boekhandelaar K. LOOS, alhier. (1267)

ER WORDT GEVRAAGD:
Eene Protestantsche MEID,
welke voorzien is van goede Getuigen, omtrent haar vlug en zindelijk Werk, zedelijk gedrag en goed kunnende Koken, liefst niet beneden de 26 jaren. Adres met franco Brieven, onder het Nommer dezer Advertentie, aan het Bureau dezer Courant. (1258)

TEGEN MEI WORDT GEVRAAGD:
EENE KINDERMEID,
van de P. G., die van goede Getuigenissen voorzien is: Adres bij den Boekhandelaar P. M. BAZENDIJK, aan de Leuvehaven. (1247)

ER BIEDT ZICH AAN, om terstond in dienst te treden: Een
ONDER-KINDERMEISJE,
achttien jaar oud, van de P. G. en van goede Getuigen voorzien. Adres aan het Bureau dezer Courant. (1353)

Figure 2: Two columns of advertisements in Nieuwe Rotterdamsche Courant (15-2-1854) that are identified as a single advertisement.

Job ads were extracted based on an expansive list of occupations obtained from the historical international classification of occupations (HISCO) database (Mandemakers et al., 2019; van Leeuwen et al., 2002).[2] We considered expanding the list by generating spelling alternatives based on string edit distance (e.g. "bakcer" and "dakker" as a way to detect wrongly OCR'ed instances of "bakker"). However, this introduced a new type of noise to the dataset because these alternatives contain many words that are no longer connected to the occupation title. Moreover, the list obtained from the HISCO dataset already includes 12,671 unique occupation titles.

After selecting the advertisements based on the list of occupation titles the problem of wrongly segmented advertisements was circumvented by selecting a specific window of words around the occupation title. This introduced the problem of multiple advertisements being grouped together. However, by measuring the average number of words between occupation titles, trying different window sizes and close readings of individual advertisements we found a window of twelve words to the left, and forty words to the right of the occupation title to be the most effective. Overall, this method would result in 175,209 extracted windows on a total of 1,515,179 advertisements.

4.2. Extracting Wage Information

Information about wages and compensations for advertised occupations in nineteenth-century job advertisements comes in two forms. First, many jobs are advertised with reference to qualitative indicators such as *hoog loon* ("high pay") and *behoorlijk salaris* ("reasonable salary"). This category is also marked by wage indicators that are related to the applicants' capabilities. Especially the phrase *loon naar bekwaamheden* ("wage by capabilities") frequently appears in the advertisements in the period 1850-1870. The second category of wage information is quantitative information. Despite the 'messiness' of digitized advertisements, numerical wage indicators are relatively consistent in form. Low-skilled jobs were often paid the same: a hundred guilders a year or two guilders a week. This reflects in the advertisements. Furthermore, OCR errors are also relatively consistent. Often, "10" is recognized as "lo" and the guilder sign "ƒ" is frequently recognized as an "f". The classifier is therefore designed in such a way that the most frequently occurring OCR-errors are recognized and corrected.

4.2.1. Extracting Qualitative Wages

Qualitative wage classifiers were extracted using a list of frequently occurring indicators (such as "good wage", "wage by capabilities", "good salary" etc.). This list was composed manually on the basis of an extensive close reading exercise. We observed how only a limited range of qualitative indicators were used in the advertisements and that the use of a manually composed vocabulary of indicator was justified. Of course, OCR might have affected the identification of the indicators, but because all of the indi-

[2] `https://datasets.iisg.amsterdam/dataset.xhtml?persistentId=hdl:10622/MUZMAL`.

cators concerned short words, the effect of OCR-noise was minimal.

4.2.2. Extracting Numerical Wages

The extraction of the numerical wages was the central and most complex part of the project. We tackled this task by designing a rule based classifier. The reason for doing so is twofold. First, as mentioned earlier, the quantitative information appears in a relatively consistent form. Second, such an approach does not require large amounts of labeled training data.

The first step in identifying numerical wages was to extract all tokens with numerical characters and with a length of less than six and appearing in the selected context windows around occupation titles. Because a significant portion of the wages comprised the numbers 10 or 100, we also included tokens containing the character combinations "lo" and "loo" as a way to capture the most frequent OCR errors. Additionally, a separate vocabulary of spelled out numbers ("hundred", "fifty") was used to extract quantitative information in non-numerical form.

After selecting a list of wage candidates a rule-based classifier was used to determine the likelihood of the selected token expressing a wage. The classifier uses the following features:

- whether the first character of the token, or the preceding token is an "f" or "ƒ".
- whether the preceding token is the word *van* ("of") or *tegen* ("against"), since wages are often discussed as *loon van 5 gulden* ("wage of five guilders").
- whether the token that follows the numerical candidate is the word *gulden* ("guilder").
- whether one of the three words before or after the numerical candidate is either *loon* ("wage"), *salaris* ("salary"), *beloning* ("remuneration") or *jaarwedde* ("a year's wage").
- whether the first two characters of the numerical candidate are "18" or the token after the candidate is a month. In that case, the candidate is probably an indicator of time.

The features were selected on the basis of a close reading of a sample of over a hundred advertisements per decade. This showed that the appearance of job advertisements was relatively stable over time. Terms such as "salary" and "guilder" consistently appeared alongside occupation titles and the inner structure of advertisements was did not change significantly. This led us to select the above mentioned lexical features for the classifier.

5. Evaluation

The extraction and identification method was evaluated by comparing the extracted results with a set of manually annotated advertisements. A sample of 150 advertisements was drawn from the advertisements published in the years 1851, 1856, 1861, 1866, 1871, 1876 and 1881, resulting in a set of 1050 advertisements. Because at this stage we only wanted to evaluate the identification of wages and not the identification of occupations, we generated the windows using the method outlined in Section 4.. This resulted in a total of 620 job advertisements that formed the evaluation set.

The subsequent annotation procedure comprised the tagging of occupations, qualitative wage information, and quantitative wage information. In Table 2 below, all annotation options are listed. Initially, software (WebAnno) was used for annotation but given the fairly straightforward entities that needed annotation it proved much faster to use a hand-built Python script.

The following rules were set for annotating the windows:

- If two occupation titles are mentioned *reiziger of secondant* ("traveler or assistant"), both titles were annotated only if one of them is not detected in another advertisement. The script that creates the windows based on the occupations generates separate advertisement windows for every detected occupation, so in the case of "reiziger of secondant" both *reiziger* and *secondant* could have their "own" window. Therefore, if both are detected and processed as separate windows only one is annotated.
- Wages can come in the form of a range, such as: *f 100 tot f 120* ("f 100 tot f 120"). In this case, both indicators are annotated (separate by a space). However, when there is extra money to be earned *f 100 inclusief f5 waschgeld* ("f1 including f5 laundry allowance"), only the 'main' wage number is anntated.
- qualitative and quantitative information sometimes cooccurs. In that case they are annotated as: quan [token(s)], qual [token(s)].

During the annotation it turned out that half of the advertisements could either not be classified as a job advertisement, or did not contain any wage indicators. The first problem arose from occupation titles such as *boekhandelaar* ("bookseller"), or *burgemeester* ("mayor") that were mentioned in different contexts (See Figure 1). The second problem, was mostly caused by high-skilled occupations (teachers and civil servants) that were not accompanied by wages.

In Table 3 we report the results of the evaluation procedure. Because the results vary based on whether we count all ads, ads that are only classified as job ads, or ads that contain wage indicators, we differentiated the evaluation results. With f_1 scores between 0.624 and 0.724 our classifiers works reasonably well in extracting wage information. Given our original corpus of around 1.000.000 advertisements, containing around 175.000 occupations, a recall of 70% would give us 122.500 correctly classified advertisements. Here, we have to keep in mind the issue of true negatives: many of the windows are extracted on the basis of occupation titles that do not relate to job advertisements, but to other types of advertising. For example, the word "baker" could also be used in the context of bread advertisements. The classifier correctly discards these windows, because they are not job advertisements. However, in the

Feature	Tag	Situation
Occupation	[occupation title]	if the extracted occupation is correct
Occupation	"na"	if the extracted occupation is incorrect because the ad is not a job ad
Occupation	[correct occupation]	if the extracted occupation is incorrect because another occupation is advertised
Occupation	"np"	if the extracted occupation is incorrect because no occupation is mentioned
WAGE	"qual" [token(s)]	if the extracted wage is indicated by qualitative indicators
WAGE	"quan" [token]	if the extracted wage is indicated by quantitative indicators
WAGE	"na"	if no wage indicators are present because the ad is not a job ad
WAGE	"np"	if no wage indicators are present

Table 2: Explanation of the tags used in the annotation.

	All Ads	Job Ads	Ads with Indicators
precision	0.715	0.717	0.641
recall	0.754	0.737	0.607
f_1	0.734	0.727	0.624

Table 3: Evaluation results for three different categories of advertisements in the evaluation set.

evaluation process, these "true negatives" are counted as correct classifications. When translating the recall of 70% to the expected number of extracted advertisements, these true negatives must be taken into account.

6. Preview: Wages in Domestic Services

To illustrate the types of analyses a structured dataset on wages can facilitate, we include a small example here of the combined wages of four similar occupations: kitchenmaid, maid, servant and housekeeper. Figure 3 shows the extracted quantitative wage indicators in the period between 1850 and 1879, combined for all four occupations. The resulting nominal wage series is fairly flat, but for the 1850–1875 period this is in line with other work (Allen, 2001).[3]. Moreover, the variation in wages in any given year confirms that there is substantial wage heterogeneity, even within a set of similar occupations.

7. Conclusions and Future Work

In this paper, we presented an approach and experiments for extracting wages and occupations from historical newspaper ads. We highlighted the main challenges in working with non-digital born data, as well as artefacts of the digitization process such as OCR and segmentation errors. Our observations can serve as guidelines for other researchers taking on text-driven analyses on historical newspapers.

Our method of extracting information about wages and occupations in historical advertisements proves to be a promising line of research. It sheds a light on the socio-economic history of professional categories that generally lack quantitative evidence. By using large-scale digital corpora and relatively straightforward text classification methods, this evidence can be gathered.

Of course, several problems need to be resolved before we can use wage indicators as reliable quantitative evidence. Three practical problems need further attention. First, occupations need disambiguation. In the example "baker searches apprentice", both occupations, along with their windows, are extracted. In the current situation, both occupations would be connected to a wage indicator that only refers to "apprentice". Tackling this problem could be done by, for example, considering the verbs that surround a specific occupation or by simply removing occupation titles that are seldom advertised. A second problem is the occurrence of multiple quantitative indicators in the advertisements. Wages were often negotiable or dependent on capabilities or background. In that case, we might encounter "f50-60", "100, rising to 110" or "f100 with a bonus of f10 a month". Currently, the classifier selects only the "top candidate" from the ad. This problem could be resolved by a second classifier that disambiguates multiple numerical indicators extracted from the ads.

Thirdly, we could only perform an evaluation on a sample of the dataset. For large-scale data enrichments, further evaluations using different samples, or a human-in-the-loop annotation approach are recommended. Here, additional information about the system's decisions such as its confidence or the text quality can help distinguish 'easy' from 'difficult' cases, enabling a setup where human experts are only presented those cases that the computer cannot solve. We foresee many benefits from hybrid annotation efforts and hope our experiment provides a first inspiration for such experiments in different contexts.

[3]`http://www.iisg.nl/hpw/data.php#europe`

References

Allen, R. C., Bassino, J.-P., Ma, D., Moll-Murata, C., and Van Zanden, J. L. (2011). Wages, prices, and living standards in China, 1738-1925: in comparison with Europe, Japan, and India. *The Economic History Review*, 64:8–38, February.

Allen, R. C. (2001). The Great Divergence in European Wages and Prices from the Middle Ages to the First World War. *Explorations in Economic History*, 38(4):411–447, October.

Allen, R. C. (2009). *The British industrial revolution in global perspective*. New approaches to economic and social history. Cambridge University Press, Cambridge [etc.].

Clark, G. (2005). The Condition of the Working Class in England, 1209–2004. *Journal of Political Economy*, 113(6):1307–1340, December.

Cummins, N. (2019). Where Is the Middle Class? Inequality, Gender and the Shape of the Upper Tail from

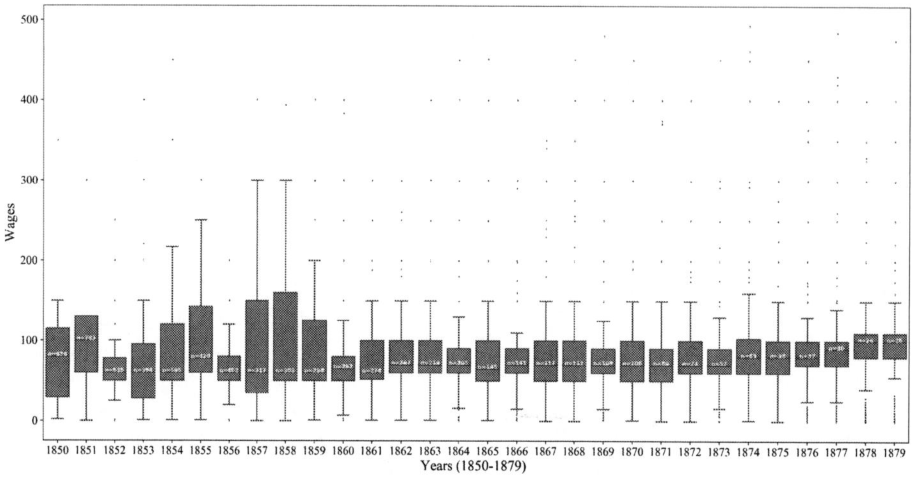

Figure 3: Box plots of quantitative wages extracted for the occupations *keukenmeid* ("kitchenmaid"), *meid* ("maid"), *huishoudster* ("housekeeper") and *bediende* ("servant") in the years between 1850 and 1879. Inside the boxplots, the number of observations for every year is included.

60 Million English Death and Probate Records, 1892-2016. Technical report, London School of Economics & Political Science (LSE).

de Zwart, P., van Leeuwen, B., and van Leeuwen-Li, J. (2014). Real wages since 1820. In *How Was Life? Global well-being since 1820*, pages 73–86. Organisation for Economic Co-operation and Development, October.

Feinstein, C. H. (1998). Pessimism Perpetuated: Real Wages and the Standard of Living in Britain during and after the Industrial Revolution. *Journal of Economic History*, 58(03):625–658.

Gray, R. (2018). Selection Bias in Historical Housing Data. Technical report, Queen's University Belfast, Belfast.

Humphries, J. and Schneider, B. (2019). Spinning the industrial revolution. *The Economic History Review*, 72(1):126–155.

Humphries, J. and Weisdorf, J. (2019). Unreal Wages? Real Income and Economic Growth in England, 1260–1850. *The Economic Journal*, 129(623):2867–2887.

Humphries, J. (2003). Child labor: Lessons from the historical experience of today's industrial economies. *The World Bank Economic Review*, 17(2):175–196.

Knigge, A. (2016). Beyond the parental generation: The influence of grandfathers and great-grandfathers on status attainment. *Demography*, 53.

Mandemakers, K., Mourits, R., and Muurling, S. (2019). HSN_hisco_release_2018_01, December. Publisher: IISH Data Collection type: dataset.

Reynaert, M. (2008). Non-interactive ocr post-correction for giga-scale digitization projects. In *International Conference on Intelligent Text Processing and Computational Linguistics*, pages 617–630. Springer.

Schulz, W., Maas, I., and van Leeuwen, M. H. D. (2014). Employer's choice – Selection through job advertisements in the nineteenth and twentieth centuries. *Research in Social Stratification and Mobility*, 36:49–68, June.

Stephenson, J. Z. (2018). 'Real' wages? Contractors, workers, and pay in London building trades, 1650–1800. *The Economic History Review*, 71(1):106–132.

van Leeuwen, M. H. D., Maas, I., and Miles, A. (2002). *HISCO: Historical international standard classification of occupations*. Leuven University Press, Leuven. OCLC: 49628570.

van Strien, D., Beelen, K., Ardanuy, M. C., Hosseini, K., McGillivray, B., and Colavizza, G. (2020). Assessing the impact of ocr quality on downstream nlp tasks. In *Proceedings of the 12th International Conference on Agents and Artificial Intelligence (ICAART 2020)*, pages 484–496, Valleta, Malta, Feb. SCITEPRESS.

Weischedel, R. and Boschee, E. (2018). What can be accomplished with the state of the art in information extraction? a personal view. *Computational Linguistics*, 44(4):651–658.

Wevers, M. (2017). *Consuming America: A Data-Driven Analysis of the United States as a Reference Culture in Dutch Public Discourse on Consumer Goods, 1890-1990*. Ph.D. thesis, University Utrecht.

Proceedings of LR4SSHOC: Workshop about Language Resources for the SSH Cloud, pages 33–36
Language Resources and Evaluation Conference (LREC 2020), Marseille, 11–16 May 2020

LR4SSHOC: The Future of Language Resources in the Context of the Social Sciences and Humanities Open Cloud

Daan Broeder[1], Maria Eskevich[1], Monica Monachini[2]
[1] CLARIN ERIC, [2] Institute of Computational Linguistics - CNR
[1] Utrecht, The Netherlands, [2] Via Moruzzi,1 – Pisa
d.g.broeder@uu.nl, maria@clarin.eu, monica.monachini@ilc.cnr.it

Abstract

This paper outlines the future of language resources and identifies their potential contribution for creating and sustaining the social sciences and humanities (SSH) component of the European Open Science Cloud (EOSC).

Keywords: Language Resources, European Open Science Cloud, Social Sciences and Humanities

1. Introduction

The term Language Resource (LR) refers to a broad type of speech and language data in machine readable form, used to study language or assist language processing applications. Examples of Language Resources are: written or spoken corpora and lexica, multi-modal resources, grammars, terminology or domain specific databases and dictionaries, ontologies, multimedia databases, etc. Language Technology (LT) are broadly defined as software tools for the analysis and use of Language.

The development of LR, LT, and their management have reached the level of maturity that allows their application to be expanded beyond the borders of traditional linguistic disciplines. In principle, such proliferation of resources and technologies is at the core of initiatives leading to the creation and building of the European Open Science Cloud (EOSC)[1]. EOSC is the latest development of the European approach to research infrastructure building. It has a long history starting with the series of ESFRI roadmaps[2].

In every field of research the steps towards EOSC have led to discussions on how to best accommodate the needs and requests of representative communities while complying with the technical requirements inherent to the implementation of EOSC.

At previous stages the ERICs (European Research Infrastructure Consortium)[3] were established to answer the need of specific research communities for infrastructure solutions. The first two to be created were SHARE[4] and CLARIN[5], both ERICs for the social sciences and humanities (SSH) domain. This early uptake illustrates the overall involvement of the SSH in shaping the European Research Infrastructure landscape.

Nowadays the SSH domain has grown a number of research infrastructures (RIs), CESSDA[6], CLARIN, DARIAH[7], ESS[8], SHARE[9], that support their domain-specific work with examples of collaboration where linguistic analysis is used to support studies into societal and cultural dynamics. Research in the broader SSH domain can benefit from language data because of the potential value of extracting information from data expressed in the form of natural language. Well organized and easy access to language resources and relevant processing tools can stimulate the broadening of research questions and the improvement of tools for the analysis of language resources.

Some SSH research infrastructures have been able to articulate their community requirements and their domain-specific agenda by participating in large e-Infrastructure projects, such as EUDAT[10], EGI[11] and EOSC-hub[12]. The latter project has integrated some key CLARIN services[13] into European Open Science Cloud (EOSC).

To foster collaboration between related research domains, the European Commission (EC) has introduced funding instruments for thematic cluster projects which are open for consortia consisting of multiple ERICs from related disciplinary fields. Cluster projects are expected to develop common solutions for similar problems and inform one-another about specific approaches.

The project Social Sciences and Humanities Open Cloud (SSHOC[14]) is such a cluster project, which is part of the series of INFRA-EOSC projects: H2020 initiatives aimed at building the EOSC, and the to creation and support of the SSH part of the EOSC via alignment and integration of infrastructural services from the Social Sciences, Humanities and Cultural Heritage. SSHOC represents the third generation of SSH cluster projects.

This paper describes the role of LR and LT in the context

[1] https://ec.europa.eu/info/publications/european-open-science-cloud-eosc-strategic-implementation-plan_en

[2] https://www.esfri.eu/esfri-roadmap

[3] For an overview of all ERICs established and the links to their websites, see the information pages of ERIC Forum on the ERIC Landscape.

[4] http://www.share-project.org

[5] https://www.clarin.eu

[6] https://www.cessda.eu

[7] https://www.dariah.eu

[8] www.europeansocialsurvey.org

[9] http://www.share-project.org

[10] https://eudat.eu

[11] https://www.egi.eu

[12] https://www.eosc-hub.eu

[13] https://www.clarin.eu/eosc

[14] https://sshopencloud.eu

of the SSH Open Cloud. Section 2 addresses the main features that define the development of research infrastructures at large are discussed. Section 3 zooms in into the specific aspects of European long-term existing initiatives that build the ground for future development. Section 4 identifies the current capacities and current difficulties in sharing and optimising research data and creating and sustaining an infrastructure for the SSH domain, and Section 5 summarises the most prominent issues and potential that will define the configuration of LR and LT in the context of EOSC.

2. Challenges of RI landscape for the SSH

As outlined in Section 1, the EC initiated EOSC that is currently rolled out in the form of a number of European Union (EU) level and regional projects. In order to understand the dynamics of such developments, it is useful to examine diverse challenges in the current research environment that influence the decision taking process, and that are expected to be tackled through EOSC. The very dynamic landscape of research infrastructure builders and service providers is influenced by a number of trends and interests:

- Data deluge: Although currently already a well described, "almost flogged to death" concept, it is still a challenging and unsolved in daily research reality, and requires the uptake of (for many) new highly performant data management solutions. (Hey and Trefethen, 2003)
- Scale up for efficiency: On the one hand, the goal to serve targeted research communities is achieved through creation and development of ERICs and thematic cluster collaborations that are expected to provide more generic services. On the other hand, the non-thematic service providers, e-Infrastructures as EGI and EUDAT that do not serve a particular community understandably tend to avoid diversification of their services.
- Professionalising service provisioning and software development: There is a trend to follow technology adoption and operational protocols from industry, as for instance the use of IT Service Management as FitSM[15] and the use of security standards as ISO 27001[16], which is in agreement with the previous point. In general this can be a beneficial development improving efficiency.
- **F**indable, **A**ccessible, **I**nteroperable and **R**eusable (Wilkinson et al., 2016): Across different research domains there is a broad agreement to adopt FAIR principles when implementing services and data management protocols as a means to ensure proper access and re-use of research data and services.

In addition to the above listed trends that can be observed across all domains, there is number of domain- and community- specific aspects of research infrastructure building that have intrinsic influence on the decisions taken:

- While there is a steady increase in technical knowledge and proficiency amongst the researchers in the field of SSH, it appears that a number of intrinsic limitations in terms of technical complexity of research software and infrastructure solutions are still in place. The SSH community as a whole does not accept high IT proficiency as a default requirement for engaging into research. For instance purely qualitative researchers usually do not make use of advanced technical solutions. In comparison to "hard sciences", it is harder to engage with and to encourage the SSH community as a whole to change the research methodologies adopting broader usage of technological solutions, and there is an urgency to make the infrastructure developers aware of the need to communicate with end-users at the appropriate level of expertise. Note that scaling-up IT support organisations will not always favour easy support and communication with end-users.
- Another aspect of current SSH infrastructures that is important to consider is the use of strong thematic centres as a backbone. This is the case for at least two RIs: CESSDA and CLARIN. These centres play an essential role within the research infrastructures, hosting data and services for their own purposes and users, but also, as in the case of for example CLARIN, contributing to the central infrastructure services. The thematic centres are largely funded by individual national governments and funding agencies and are major national contributions to the a common European infrastructure. The RIs play an important role in formulating quality and certification requirements for those centres, in accordance with EOSC policies, that they themselves helped to shape.

3. SSHOC contribution and impact

Realising the SSH part of the EOSC, means, on the one side, to make SSH data, language processing tools, and services available, adjusted and accessible for users across SSH domain and, on the other side, to align and integrate services and infrastructures from the Social Sciences, Humanities and Cultural Heritage with one another and with the now emerging EOSC.

Different perspectives on activities, contributions and results aimed at realising the SSH Open Cloud can be outlined:

- From the perspective of EC: it is important to know that the thematic cluster projects such as SSHOC were specifically intended to make a link between the EOSC development and the research communities and that cluster project play an important role in the community consultation process and EOSC governance.
- From the perspective of a thematic cluster project such as SSHOC: challenges and successes should ideally be measured by how project results can be made useful for the common good, i.e. the outcome should be useful for more than just one of the SSHOC stakeholders.

[15] https://www.fitsm.eu

[16] https://www.iso.org/isoiec-27001-information-security.html

- From the perspective of a SSHOC partner: the possibility for the individual stakeholder infrastructures to build long term partnerships and to make related initiatives known and accessible to the other SSHOC partners is important.
- From the perspective of communities that are served by RIs within the thematic cluster: there is a possibility to be represented and to have the community voice/opinion heard at the level of EOSC through SSHOC activities. For example, the larger SSH communities, such as DARIAH, E-RIHS[17], CESSDA, can benefit from CLARIN's long-term relation with the European and US Language Resource agencies, such as ELDA[18] and LDC[19] (Cieri, 2020), and CLARIN involvement in LREC community. Whereas the LREC community and representative agencies expose their resources and tools to large audiences of potential users.

As SSHOC can offer a link to and a view on how the EOSC initiative searches to transform the way research infrastructures are built and made available to researchers. This can have consequences for the way Language Resources and Technology (LRT) should be produced and made available. Thus, it can be considered as part of the CLARIN mission in SSHOC to consider and discuss such consequences for the traditional LRT centers as it should for the CLARIN centers.

While national organisations involved in CLARIN consortia and SSHOC are also participating in other European initiatives with a focus on LT, such as the industry-oriented ELG project[20], their participation in SSHOC can also contribute to a better alignment with EOSC. Thus it helps EOSC to generate further impact outside academia.

One of the benefits for the infrastructures participating in SSHOC is the sharing of infrastructure building efforts amongst partners and the potential for developing a common strategy towards the landscape dynamics and trends listed in Section 2. The possibilities for scaling up the use of infrastructure components through SSHOC is illustrated by the planned uptake of two key CLARIN infrastructure components by DARIAH, CESSDA and E-RIHS, in this case the CLARIN Language Resource Switchboard[21] and the CLARIN Virtual Collection Registry[22]. Extensive consultation between SSHOC partners takes place to guide their generalisation and find integration opportunities. Another example is that after an evaluation of the vocabulary management platforms currently used in the SSH domain and the selection of one or more common registries and a common management platform, wider visibility of agreed vocabularies are likely to be expected.

Also with respect to the creation of completely new common infrastructure components, there are two planned examples: (i) the SSH Open Marketplace mentioned below and (ii) a prototype of a SSHOC Citation infrastructure for "FAIR SSH Citations" which is intended to make citations machine-actionable.

4. Aspects of LR4SSHOC implementation

In order to bring the LR to the SSH Open Cloud diverse aspects of implementation are to be taken into account.

4.1. Findability of services and solutions

Although the need for stable well defined data management and processing services for research cannot be denied, equally or even more important is the need for flexibility and short turn-around with regard to implementation of new requirements and adaptation of for instance natural language processing (NLP) software and workflows to new insights emerging in scholarly practises or from thematic research agendas. In such cases the current solutions for service registration and evaluation offered by the EOSC solutions, the EOSC catalogue and EOSC Marketplace are probably too inflexible for the integration of domain-specific services, and clearly more suited for generic data management services that are typically very stable. However, registration of services is crucial for wider visibility, and therefore, it is important to enable registration for the often more dynamically developing class of domain-specific research software. Not only for sharing amongst researchers but also for acknowledgement and visibility by funding agencies. However, service registration would be more effective if the agency is closer to the research communities that may be also better positioned to contextualise the registered services in terms of solutions for specific research problems. SSHOC is developing the SSH Open Marketplace also to address this need of explicit registered services in a community-managed fashion. Obviously, such thematic service and solution registries will require proper funding and especially sufficient editorial support by the communities.

4.2. Interoperability

Interoperability of data and services is the holy grail in many research infrastructure plans. Within the SSH, the interoperability with respect to data formats is probably the more easy goal to achieve, as the RIs focusing on LT and LR in the SSH context (CLARIN and DARIAH) already have adopted international standards for the use of important data formats and shape jointly the common standards, such as Text Encoding Initiative (TEI)[23] and other annotation formats. However, with respect to solving semantic interoperability, still some major controversies exist, especially with regard to the possibility to achieve uniformity in metadata descriptions and content markup. There is a large group that would work towards a universal ontology that should be applicable in all the SSH domains (and beyond) while others, would rather use pragmatic mappings between parts of different descriptive schema and vocabularies where possible and needed, referring to the huge effort involved in the maintenance of such universal ontologies. In SSHOC the pragmatic approach has been chosen, recommending schema and vocabularies on the basis

[17]http://www.e-rihs.eu

[18]http://www.elra.info

[19]https://www.ldc.upenn.edu

[20]https://www.european-language-grid.eu

[21]https://switchboard.clarin.eu

[22]http://vlo.clarin.eu

[23]https://tei-c.org/release/doc/tei-p5-doc/en/html/

of actual usage, while accepting that others need to work towards new descriptive systems and providing mappings between them. Creating and maintaining specific semantic interoperability solutions (mappings) requires domain expertise and is better done in the context of community organisation collaborations such as SSHOC. However offering a platform that allows easy management and sharing of such mapping solutions can be provided at the EOSC level since such a platform can be domain-agnostic.

5. Concluding remarks and discussion points

The future of LR and LT in the SSH part of EOSC will be partly determined by a number of policies and actions that will be shaped by the many-fold ongoing and envisaged SSHOC activities that are focused on services that can be applied to LR.

- For various reasons it is more effective to have new communities participating in and contributing to EOSC through existing cluster networks such as SSHOC instead of directly via EOSC.
- SSHOC has already successfully demonstrated the potential for sharing and scaling-up infrastructure components.
- SSHOC can play a role in aligning centres from the broader LR community with EOSC, including their industry-oriented activities.
- The desired efficiency in provision of generic services for the SSH community can often be achieved through the collaboration between research community organisations that directly share solutions rather than through the use of services of large service provider organisations.
- In large-scale collaborative projects a pragmatic approach to semantic interoperability solutions is more effective than a single ontology-oriented approaches.
- Especially in the SSH case, where a majority of researchers is less IT-savvy than in the "hard sciences", the communities are better positioned to describe and explain services and solutions.
- SSHOC collaboration will encourage sharing of infrastructure services and components across SSH domains and communities.

In order to achieve the prominent role of the communities both in infrastructure development and maintenance, as is argued and proposed in this position paper, it is paramount that long-term funding schemes and policies are in place to support shared resources and services, and that a proper community-oriented governance layer be set up.

6. Acknowledgements

The work reported here has received funding (through CLARIN ERIC) from the European Union's Horizon 2020 research and innovation programme under grant agreement No 823782 for project SSHOC. We would like to thank Franciska de Jong for providing valuable feedback and engaging the authors in exciting discussions.

7. Bibliographical References

Cieri, C. (2020). Stretching disciplinary boundaries in language resource development and use: a linguistic data consortium position paper.

Hey, A. J. G. and Trefethen, A. E. (2003). The Data Deluge: An e-Science Perspective. In F Berman, et al., editors, *Grid Computing - Making the Global Infrastructure a Reality*, pages 809–824. Wiley and Sons. Chapter: 36.

Wilkinson, M. D., Dumontier, M., Aalbersberg, I. J., Appleton, G., Axton, M., Baak, A., Blomberg, N., Boiten, J.-W., da Silva Santos, L. B., Bourne, P. E., et al. (2016). The fair guiding principles for scientific data management and stewardship. *Scientific data*, 3.

Proceedings of LR4SSHOC: Workshop about Language Resources for the SSH Cloud, pages 37–38
Language Resources and Evaluation Conference (LREC 2020), Marseille, 11–16 May 2020

EOSC as a game-changer in the Social Sciences and Humanities research activities

Donatella Castelli
Istituto di Scienza e Tecnologie dell'Informazione "A. Faedo"
Consiglio Nazionale delle Ricerche
Via Moruzzi,1 – Pisa
donatella.castelli@isti.cnr.it

Abstract

This paper aims to give some insights on how the European Open Science Cloud (EOSC) will be able to influence the Social Sciences and Humanities (SSH) sector, thus paving the way towards innovation. Points of discussion on how the LRs and RIs community can contribute to the revolution in the practice of research areas are provided.

Keywords: European Open Science Cloud, Social Sciences and Humanities

1. Research and technological progress

Research strongly influences, but is also largely influenced by, technological and societal progress. This is true for all the research domains, including the Social Science and Humanities (SSH) ones. So far, research activities in these domains have been primarily based on scattered data collected in long-lasting campaigns and analyzed by the researchers that have collected them. In the last few years, with the advent of big data, often gathered by sensors or through citizen scientist activities, and with the spreading of data innovative analysis techniques, mainly based on artificial intelligence, the situation has started to rapidly change.

2. The European Open Science Cloud

In the near future, many more changes are expected to occur thanks to the European Open Science Cloud (EOSC). With its technological, capacity and governance components, EOSC fits into this already rapidly evolving context, paving the way for a real revolution in the practice of research areas. It is will provide a trusted system giving seamless access to data and interoperable services. Through EOSC the researchers will have access to functionality supporting the whole research data cycle, from discovery and mining to storage, management, analysis and re-use across borders and disciplines.

3. Accessible datasets and services

EOSC is currently being built as a collective effort by relying on existing components, e.g. infrastructures, services, and data resources. Through its system, it will be able to perform functions and carry out purposes that do not reside in any component alone (aka emergent behavior[1]). A large part of these functions will be dedicated to supporting cross-domain and cross-sector activities and, in particular, to make accessible and exploitable datasets and services across borders.

This latter EOSC functionality is likely the one that will produce more innovation in the SSH sector. It will not only allow researchers to access similar complementary datasets collected by others. It will make it possible to enrich these datasets with contextual information in space and time using datasets and services produced in other domains, such as, for example, earth observation, environment, and medicine, just to mention a few. At the same time, researchers in the SSH sector will be able to make their outcomes available to researchers of other domains in a short time and with limited effort. This will widen the diffusion and impact of their research products, not only in the context of the research community, but also to decision-makers and innovators.

4. Removing the language barriers

In order for this vision to fully realize, EOSC will have to necessarily offer functionalities able to remove barriers in the usage of data and services. As emerged in a recent workshop organized by the EOSCSecretariat.eu project[2] dedicated to collect the needs and requirements for future research environments[3], among the barriers "language and communication" are perceived as top ones by many researchers. For example, even searching in the EOSC catalogues of services and data may not be simple. The language used for the descriptions of these resources can be really problematic for those that do not belong to the same domain and sector. For removing these language and communication barriers EOSC should include, at its core, a variety of "translation" services.

The richer these services will be, the better EOSC will be able to reach its cross-border objectives. These core services might include, for example,

(i) human to machine and machine to human translations services,

(ii) horizontal translation services able to convert domain-specific technical terms of research outputs across disciplines or to policymakers,

[1] Crawley, E. F., Cameron, B. G., and Selva, D. (2016) System Architecture: Strategy and Product Development for Complex Systems, Pearson.

[2] http://eoscsecretariat.eu/

[3] Report on the Workshop "Co-creating the EOSC: Needs and requirements for future research environments", DOI 10.5281/zenodo.3701193.

(iii) vertical translation services covering the translation of research specific concepts, as well as the explanations for different career stages, i.e. from specialists to early career researchers, students, and the interested public at large.

5. LRs and RIs contribution

If on the one hand it is indisputable that the availability of these services largely influence the impact of EOSC in revolutionizing the research practices of the SSH community, on the other hand, it is also clear that the community itself, and in particular that part of it dealing with language resources (LRs), can contribute to the realization of these services by sharing their expertise and resources.
This clearly exemplifies the role of the Research Infrastructures (RIs) in EOSC that are called to both exploit but also to contribute to it.

Proceedings of LR4SSHOC: Workshop about Language Resources for the SSH Cloud, pages 39–41
Language Resources and Evaluation Conference (LREC 2020), Marseille, 11–16 May 2020

Stretching Disciplinary Boundaries in Language Resource Development and Use: a Linguistic Data Consortium Position Paper

Christopher Cieri
University of Pennsylvania, Linguistic Data Consortium
3600 Market Street, Philadelphia, PA 19104 USA
{ccieri}@ldc.upenn.edu

Abstract

Given the persistent gap between demand and supply, the impetus to reuse language resources is great. Researchers benefit from building upon the work of others including reusing data, tools and methodology. Such reuse should always consider the original intent of the language resource and how that impacts potential reanalysis. When the reuse crosses disciplinary boundaries, the re-user also needs to consider how research standards that differ between social science and humanities on the one hand and human language technologies on the other might lead to differences in unspoken assumptions. Data centers that aim to support multiple research communities have a responsibility to build bridges across disciplinary divides by sharing data in all directions, encouraging re-use and re-sharing and engaging directly in research that improves methodologies.

Keywords: language resources, social sciences and humanities, data centers

1. Introduction

Disciplinary boundaries organize research around shared bodies of knowledge and methods, build consensus, impose order on investigative behavior and create communities of use for purposes of sharing experience (to different degrees in different disciplines). However, given the shortage of Language Resources (LRs), it is frequently necessary to look beyond the traditional disciplinary borders in order to locate data and tools to support modern research. In fact, a deeper look shows that the divisions between academic disciplines have always been porous where the creation of LRs is concerned.

The Linguistic Data Consortium's (LDC) mission since 1992 has been to provide LRs to multiple research communities for purposes of language related education research and technology development. Over that time, LDC has avoided limiting its operations by economic sector, language, geographic region, or academic discipline. LDC supports research communities in three principal ways: 1) publishing corpora from community members to give the data wider use, 2) creating new data sets of value to the community, 3) partnering with members of the research community in new research and providing service via scientific advisory boards, conference program committees and funding panels.

2. Challenges in Data Reuse

Notwithstanding the need and intent to share data across disciplinary boundaries, a potential user of 'found data' must recognize that most corpora have been designed to support specific research agendas. There are exceptions such as the 'national corpora' (e.g. the British National Corpus[1]) that document the state of a language in a specific place and time. However, the focus of data collection effort toward a specific research question may affect its suitability for other uses. A lexicon designed to support machine translation (MT) may contain all the surface forms that appear in a corpus with their glosses into a target language. Another lexicon for the same source language, designed to support speech-to-text (STT) technologies would contain pronunciations rather than glosses. Neither matches the format traditionally used in language teaching where dictionaries are typically organized by a citation form and often contain long form definitions and example sentences in addition to glosses and pronunciations. Could lexicons developed for MT or STT be used in a language teaching situation? Possibly, though that would require either adaptability on the part of the user or adaptation of the LR itself. Student users might find the organization of a dictionary by the actual forms occurring in text more convenient as it removes from them the need to determine the dictionary form. The counter argument that this would cause a ballooning of the size of the dictionary is less important for digital users. Possible augmentations, beyond adding the definitions and example sentences, might include indexing surface forms to citation forms that link to the remainder or the lexical entry. An example of such an approach appears in §5.

This need to enhance a data prior to reuse is not limited to interdisciplinary research (Graff, Bird 2000) describe the long chain of additions, modifications and re-use of two corpora well-known to HLT developers: Switchboard and TDT. The also enumerate the problem that arise when corpus development 'forks' creating multiple versions that are then augmented and used independently.

3. Datasets Created by Social Science and Humanities Researchers

Despite differences in theory, methods and access to resources among the sciences, engineering, social sciences and humanities (SSH), the history of LR development contains multiple example of cross-disciplinary teams and innovative research applying some of the current method of large scale, computational analysis of speech and text among research groups otherwise considered to belong to SSH disciplines.

One of the first publications released by LDC, the HCRC Map Task corpus (LDC93S12), was described as "*a uniquely valuable resource for speech recognition research*" (Anderson, et al. 1991, Thompson et al. 1993) by its creators who described themselves: "*The group which designed and collected the corpus covers a wide range of interests and the corpus reflects this, providing a*

[1] http://www.natcorp.ox.ac.uk/

resource for studies of natural dialogue from many different perspectives." Indeed they worked in research groups named Human Communication, Artificial Intelligence, Cognitive Science, Linguistics and Psychology and were funded by the British Economic and Social Research Council.

Among the ~34 datasets in the LDC datasets that might be called 'lexical', most were designed to support some HLT. However there are several whose intended uses include language teaching or language documentation: Hal Schiffman's English Dictionary of the Tamil Verb (LDC2009L01), Moussa Bamba's dictionaries of Bambara (LDC2016L01), Maninka (LDC2013L01) and Mawu (LDC2005L01), Steven Bird's dictionary of Dschang (LDC2003L01) and Yiwola Awoyale's Global Yoruba Lexical Database (LDC2008L03).

Phoneticians, dialectologists and sociolinguists have also contributed data to LDC in order to reach a broader audience. These include the Digital Archive of Southern Speech - NLP Version (LDC2016S05), the transcribed SLX Corpus of Classic Sociolinguistic Interviews (LDC2003T15) and the Nationwide Speech Project (LDC2007S15) which include words and sentences read under experimental conditions.

4. Reuse of Corpora in SSH

Corpora developed for HLT development have been used successfully in numerous SSH projects. Yaeger-Dror, Hall-Lew and Deckert (2002) select data from numerous publicly available corpora, including 4 from LDC, to correlate negation strategies with dialect, genre and stance. Although the authors were able to build upon the work of many corpus creators, as the paper makes clear, the researcher retains responsibility for understanding the original data, selecting corpora or parts of corpora carefully, augmenting the existing metadata and annotation and anticipating the impact of corpus features on possible analyses. For example, in their analysis of journalistic prose, the authors could draw from many millions of words of news text but decided to select balanced, representative samples of different American regions and match them with other forms of the genre. The news text included bylines but the researchers needed to find the biographies of those writers to determine if they were appropriate exemplars of the dialect regions under study.

5. Research in Social Sciences and Humanities

The use of LRs in language related research, education and technology development has evolved continuously over the past 40 years. Areas of inquiry considered impractical during the US "funding winter" enjoyed a subsequent period significant investment (Liberman 2011, 2015, Church 2017) that continues today and has yielded the successes in multiple HLTs that have in turn enabled their use in SSH research. Others are declared to be solved problems but them subsequently discovered to present unmet challenges (Xu et al. 2019, Cieri et al. 2018, Ryant et al. 2019). The emergence of new tools and methods create opportunities for SSH disciplines to adopt big data approaches. The most efficient of these build upon prior data intensive research including some undertaken outside the discipline. Making connections among research communities to share data and methods is an activity where data centers have a role if not responsibility.

Yuan and Liberman (2008) selected a large sample of US Supreme Court Oral arguments and transcripts provided by the OYEZ[2] project, applied forced-alignment to time-stamp each utterance as to where it occurs in the audio and applied diarization technology to identify the speaker in each case. These technologies increase public access to the deliberations of the court.

Another area where HLT-driven innovation has potential for wide benefit is in language teaching. In Arabic, learning to read presents challenges resulting from the diglossia, dialect diversity, morphological complexity and orthographic features of the language. Digital dictionaries and morphological analysis can offer the learner insights into the language as well as freedom from some of the inefficiencies of traditional study. LDC's Arabic Reading Enhancement Tool (Maamouri 2009) facilitates learner access to standard learner texts through morphological analysis, parsing, digital lexicon and speech synthesis. When learners click on a word in text, that surface form which may be highly inflected or irregular and written without diacritics is indexed to its dictionary form, the relevant dictionary entry is displayed and the word is optionally diacritized and read aloud synthetically.

Other LDC research in SSH disciplines includes work to increase the empirical robustness of assessing film audience engagement. LDC's James Fiumara and Penn Professor of Cinema Studies and English Peter Decherny are co-PIs on "*Measuring Fan Engagement: Finding and Quantifying Text Reuse in Fan Fiction*". The project created the Fan Engagement Meter[3] presenting visualizations of the re-use of text from movie scripts in fan fiction. To date the site covers the Star Wars, The Hobbit/Lord of the Rings and Harry Potter film franchises. The visualization represents the script on the horizontal axis and degree of reuse on the vertical. Hovering over any part of the visualization displays the relevant portion of the text, shaded to show degree of reuse. Researchers can chose to display reuse as a function of exact or fuzzy match and can overlay plots of dialog by character and of sentiment analysis of the script to explore the relations among character, emotion and engagement.

More recent work includes research on the prosodic correlates of sermonic speech in poetry (Mustazza 2019). In this work, the datasets include the text and audio of readings of poetry that have been time aligned and subsequently analyzed for linguistic features that covary with human classification of the style of reading.

6. Conclusion

Linguistic data centers have an obligation to promote the responsible reuse of LRs whether created for HLT or SSH (or other) research and whether used within or across disciplines. Data centers can meet these obligations by engaging with research communities to offer access to existing data, encourage data sharing, document corpus features that affect reuse and take part directly in research that provide proof of concept and improvements to methodology.

[2] https://www.oyez.org/

[3] https://fanengagement.org

7. Bibliographical References

Anderson, Anne H.; Bader, Miles; Bard, Ellen Gurman; Boyle, Elizabeth; Doherty, Gwyneth; Garrod, Simon; Isard, Stephen; Kowtko, Jacqueline; McAllister, Jan; Miller, Jim; Sotillo, Catherine; Thompson, Henry S.; Weinert, Regina (1991) The HCRC Map Task Corpus. *Language and Speech*, 34(4):351-366.

Church, Kenneth (2017) Emerging trends: A tribute to Charles Wayne, *Natural Language Engineering* 24(1): 155-160.

Cieri, Christopher, Mark Liberman, Stephanie Strassel, Denise DiPersio, Jonathan Wright, Andrea Mazzucchi, James Fiumara (2018) From 'Solved Problems' to New Challenges: A Report on LDC Activities. Proc. Language Resources and Evaluation Conference, pp. 3265-3269.

Graff, David, Steven Bird (2000) Many uses, many annotations for large speech corpora: Switchboard and TDT as case studies. Proceedings of the Second International Conference on Language Resources and Evaluation, pp. 427-433, Paris: European Language Resources Association.

Liberman, Mark (2011) Lessons for Reproducible Science from the DARPA Speech and Language Program, presented at the AAAS Workshop: The Digitization of Science: Reproducibility and Interdisciplinary Knowledge Transfer, February 17-21, Washington, DC.

Liberman, Mark (2015) Reproducible Research and the Common Task Method, Simons Foundation Lectures, https://www.simonsfoundation.org/event/reproducible-research-and-the- common-task-method.

Mohammed, Mohamed (2009) LDC Arabic Reading Tools: "Read to Succeed" ACTFL 2009: Arabic SIG Meeting, San Diego, CA, November 21.

Mustazza, Chris (2019) In Search of the Sermonic: Hearing Sonic Genre in Poetry Recordings, presented at Plotting Poetry (and Poetics) 3 - Machiner la poésie (et la poétique) 3, 26-27 Sept. 2019, ATILF, Nancy, France.

Ryant, Neville, Kenneth Church, Christopher Cieri, Alejandrina Cristia, Jun Du, Sriram Ganapathy, Mark Liberman (2019) The Second DIHARD Diarization Challenge: Dataset, task, and baselines. In Proceedings Interspeech, September 15–19, 2019, Graz, Austria, pp, 978-982.

Thompson, Henry S., Anne Anderson, Ellen Gurman Bard, Gwyneth Doherty-Sneddon, Alison Newlands, and Cathy Sotillo. (1993) The HCRC Map Task corpus: natural dialogue for speech recognition. Proceedings of the workshop on Human Language Technology (HLT '93). Association for Computational Linguistics, USA, pages 25–30.

Xu, T., Zhang, H., & Zhang, X. (2019) Joint Training ResCNN-based Voice Activity Detection with Speech Enhancement. In 2019 Asia-Pacific Signal and Information Processing Association Annual Summit and Conference (APSIPA ASC) 1157-1162, IEEE.

Yaeger-Dror, Malcah Lauren Hall-Lew, Sharon Deckert (2002) It's not or isn't it? Using large corpora to determine the influences on contraction strategies. Language Variation and Change 14:79–118.

Yuan, Jiahong, Mark Liberman (2008) Speaker Identification on The Scotus Corpus, Proceedings of Acoustics, pp. 5687-90.

Proceedings of LR4SSHOC: Workshop about Language Resources for the SSH Cloud, pages 42–44
Language Resources and Evaluation Conference (LREC 2020), Marseille, 11–16 May 2020

Crossing the SSH Bridge with Interview Data

Henk van den Heuvel
CLS/CLST, Radboud University
Erasmusplein 1, Nijmegen, the Netherlands
h.vandenheuvel@let.ru.nl

Abstract

Spoken audio data, such as interview data, is a scientific instrument used by researchers in various disciplines crossing the boundaries of social sciences and humanities. In this paper, we will have a closer look at a portal designed to perform speech-to-text conversion on audio recordings through Automatic Speech Recognition (ASR) in the CLARIN infrastructure. Within the cluster cross-domain EU project SSHOC the potential value of such a linguistic tool kit for processing spoken language recording has found uptake in a webinar about the topic, and in a task addressing audio analysis of panel survey data. The objective of this contribution is to show that the processing of interviews as a research instrument has opened up a fascinating and fruitful area of collaboration between Social Sciences and Humanities (SSH).

Keywords: SSH, interview data, automatic speech recognition, NLP, spoken language processing

1. Introduction: Cross Disciplinary Use of Interview Data

Spoken audio data, such as interview data, is a scientific instrument used by researchers in various disciplines. These disciplines span the social sciences and the humanities. An oral historian will typically approach a recorded interview as an intersubjective account of a past experience, whereas another historian might consider the same source of interest only because of the factual information it conveys. A social scientist is likely to try to discover common themes and similarities and differences across a whole set of interviews, whereas a computational linguist will rely on counting frequencies and detecting collocations and co-occurrences, for similar purposes. On the other hand sociologists who interview, often seek to understand their interviewees in the same way as (oral) historians (Scagliola et al., 2020).

Then the question arises how the various disciplines can benefit from the large amount of freely available transcription, annotation, linguistic and emotion recognition tools. We should take into account that most scholars are not familiar with each other's approaches, and hesitate to take up technology. When software is used, it is often proprietary and binds scholars to a particular set of practices.

To clear the situation a multidisciplinary international community of experts organised a series of hands-on workshops with scholars who work with interview data, and tested the reception of a number of digital tools that are used at various stages of the research process. We engaged with tools for transcription, for annotation, for analysis and for emotion recognition. The workshops were held at Oxford, Utrecht, Arezzo, Munich, Utrecht and Sofia between 2016 and 2019, and were mostly sponsored by CLARIN. Participants were recruited among communities of historians, social science scholars, linguists, speech technologists, phonologists, archivists and information scientists. The website https://oralhistory.eu/ was set up to communicate across disciplinary borders. For a full account of experiences, we refer to Scagliola et al., (2020).

Through these workshops it became ever clearer that, despite different scientific methods of analysis used by these researchers, core processing methods of this kind of data are cross-disciplinary. Creating transcriptions with appropriate level of detail is one of the initial and most important steps in the spoken audio data analysis, but this step can also be very time-consuming. This is why researchers can greatly benefit from at least partial automation of the transcription process. However, choosing high-quality tools and learning how to use them is not always a straightforward process, and researchers can quickly lose their enthusiasm for automation for the fear of that the automation process might be too complex or non-transparent.

In this paper, we will have a closer look at a portal designed to perform speech-to-text conversion on audio recordings of interviews through Automatic Speech Recognition (ASR) with an option to manually correct the text output (section 2). Then we will point to a number of options to apply NLP analysis tools to the resulting text (section 3), and finally we will address activities organized in the SSHOC project[1] to set up a bridge spanning the SSH communities using ASR for recorded audio materials (section 4).

2. Interview Data and ASR

Automatic speech recognition (ASR) has reached a performance level where, under favorable acoustic conditions, a quality of transcriptions can be achieved that is a sufficient starting point for many researchers to start subsequent (domain specific) text analysis (labelling and encoding on). An additional advantage of using ASR for transcription purposes is that the output comes with time stamps of the words locating them in the original audio

1 https://sshopencloud.eu/

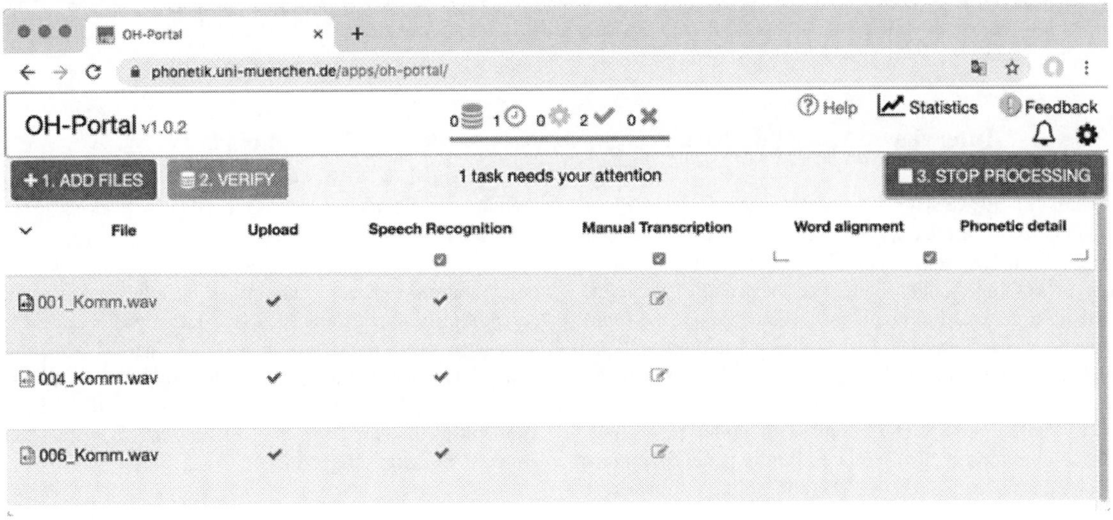

Figure 1. Screenshot of OH Portal with three audio files. The files were uploaded and processed by ASR, and are now awaiting manual correction of the transcript.

stream and permitting seamless subtitling of audio and video recordings.

Draxler et al. (2020) describe a webportal developed for the CLARIN ERIC[2] where researchers can upload audio recordings, use ASR engines for a variety of languages to obtain text transcriptions of the recordings, and to manually correct the transcriptions and realign the corrected transcripts with the audio files. The portal is accessible via a login at https://clarin.phonetik.uni-muenchen.de/apps/oh-portal/. Upon entering the portal the user sees the screen depicted in Figure 1, showing the three phases in the transcription process mentioned above. Draxler et al. (2020) gives a detailed account of the various processing steps, the user agreements for the available speech recognisers (also with respect to privacy issues), the technical limitations of the portal, the performance one may expect, and guidelines for making audio recordings that are suitable for ASR processing.

3. From ASR output to NLP

As pointed out in Draxler et al. (2020) we are well aware of the relevance of tools for follow up analyses after the speech to text conversion in the portal. The current workflow implemented by the OH portal is derived from the requirements of speech technology development. However, the requirements of oral historians but also of humanities scholars and social scientists are different. Studying the interaction between two people who construct meaning via a dialogue, requires retrieving high-level information from the recordings, it is not only about 'what is said' but also about 'how it is said'. Scholars want to know: what is the major topic of the recording, what emotions can be observed, what are the named entities, what can be said about the regional background of the speaker, what relationships exist between historical data and audio recordings, etc. Trained human transcribers may extract this information, but this is a time-consuming manual process. Topic modelling, sentiment analysis, named entity recognition, dialect modelling and information extraction or summarization are all active research areas in computational linguistics and speech processing.

In Scagliola et al. (2020) we presented an overview of NLP analysis packages used in the workshops. These include lemmatizers, syntactic parsers, named entity recognizers, auto-summarizers, tools for detecting concordances/n-grams and semantic correlations. Participants were then given a live demo of the software tools and then some step by step guided exercises with data. Linguistic tools introduced were

- Voyant (https://voyant-tools.org/), a lightweight text analysis tool that yields output on the fly
- the Stanford CoreNLP (https://stanfordnlp.github.io/CoreNLP/), a linguistic tool that can automatically tag words in a number of different ways, such as recognizing part of speech, type of proper noun, numeric quantities, and more
- Autosummarizer (http://autosummarizer.com/), a website which uses AI to automatically produce summaries of texts.
- TXM, a more complex tool for 'textometry', a methodology allowing quantitative and qualitative analysis of textual corpora, by combining developments in lexometric and statistical research with corpus technologies (http://textometrie.ens-lyon.fr/?lang=en). It allows for a more granular analysis of language features, requiring the integration of a specific language model, the splitting of speakers, the conversion of data into computer readable XML language, and the lemmatization of the data.

2 http://clarin.eu/

4. Interviews, ASR and SSHOC

Within the EU SSHOC[3] project (which is focused on cooperation of the SSH communities in sharing data and tools) the potential value of CLARIN's linguistic tool kit for processing spoken language recording has found uptake in general in organizing webinars about the topic, and more specifically in Task 4.4 which addresses *Voice recorded interviews and audio analysis*. In this task we aim to introduce specific questions LISS Panel surveys to which participants can respond with audio recordings. These questions typically relate to more general opinions on for instance finances, ethics, and politics. A use case will be started for Dutch in which the audio recordings will be transcribed using the Dutch ASR and processed using further NLP tools such as for summarization, topic detection and, possibly, automatic translation. Special care will be given to GDPR compliant data collection and processing (Emery et al., 2019).

In order to raise awareness for the potential benefits of ASR for the transcription of audio recordings a webinar was organized by the dissemination team of SSHOC in which the background of the portal was addressed, followed by a tutorial on how to use it. A blogpost[4] about the webinar was published together with a Youtube podcast[5].

There were 172 viewers of the webinar. The majority of participants came from the EU countries, but the webinar was also followed by some participants from countries outside Europe (i.e. the USA, several African countries, China, etc.). The great majority (approx. 70 %), belonged to categories "Researchers, Research Networks and Communities" and "Universities and research performing institutions". These two categories were followed by "Research libraries and archives", "Research and e-infrastructures" and "Private sector and industry players". Their representation accounted to approximately 20 % of the entire audience. The remaining categories, "Policy making organizations", "Research funding organizations" and "Civil society and citizen scientists" were represented only by a few participants (approx. 10 %). These numbers show the enormous interest for and potential of spoken language processing in a wide variety of scientific disciplines.

As a follow up of the webinar we started organising four weekly QA sessions during which users of the OH portal can contact us in an interactive session based on pre-submitted issues that they come up e.g. in using the portal for their research.

3 https://sshopencloud.eu/

4 https://www.sshopencloud.eu/news/sshoc-webinar-clarin-hands-tutorial-transcribing-interview-data

5 https://www.youtube.com/watch?v=X6bFGJpMjVQ&t=6s

5. Conclusion

Our experiences with the various workshops and the webinar have convinced the Oral History working group (see section 1) that the processing of interviews as a research instrument has opened up a fascinating area of collaboration between humanities scholars and social scientists. Research tools such as the OH portal appear to appeal to great variety of researchers across academic disciplines. Building the appropriate tools requires a lot of "overbridging" talk by ICT developers in the Digital Humanities, but the fruits we see growing from that tree are certainly worth the efforts.

6. Bibliographical References

Draxler, C., Van den Heuvel. H., Van Hessen, A., Calamai, S., Corti, L., Scagliola, S. (2020). A CLARIN Transcription Portal for Interview Data. *Proceedings of the 12th International Conference on Language Resources and Evaluation (LREC2020).*

Emery, T., Luijckx, R., Vanden Heuvel, H., (2019). Guidelines for the integration of Audio Capture data in Survey Interviews. *D4.12 of the SSHOC project.* https://zenodo.org/record/3631169#.Xo2N3_0za70

Scagliola, S., Corti, L., Calamai, S., Karrouche, N., Beeken, J., Van Hessen, A., Draxler, C., Van den Heuvel, H., and Broekhuizen M., (2020) Cross disciplinary overtures with interview data: Integrating digital practices and tools in the scholarly workflow. *Proceedings CLARIN Annual Conference, Leipzig, October 2019.*

Van den Heuvel, H., Draxler, C., Van Hessen, A., Corti, L., Scagliola, S., Calamai, S., Karouche, N. (2019). A Transcription Portal for Oral History Research and Beyond. *Digital Humanities 2019, Utrecht, 9-12 July 2019.* https://dev.clariah.nl/files/dh2019/boa/0854.html

Association for Computational Linguistics
209 N. Eighth Street
Stroudsburg, Pennsylvania 18360

ISBN 978-1-7138-1267-8

CURRAN ASSOCIATES INC. proceedings.com